MY FIRST LOVE LETTER

Poetry of Madathil Rajendran Nair Vol. 2

MADATHIL RAJENDRAN NAIR

Copyright © Madathil Rajendran Nair

All Rights Reserved.

This book has been self-published with all reasonable efforts taken to make the material error-free by the author. No part of this book shall be used, reproduced in any manner whatsoever without written permission from the author, except in the case of brief quotations embodied in critical articles and reviews.

The Author of this book is solely responsible and liable for its content including but not limited to the views, representations, descriptions, statements, information, opinions and references ["Content"]. The Content of this book shall not constitute or be construed or deemed to reflect the opinion or expression of the Publisher or Editor. Neither the Publisher nor Editor endorse or approve the Content of this book or guarantee the reliability, accuracy or completeness of the Content published herein and do not make any representations or warranties of any kind, express or implied, including but not limited to the implied warranties of merchantability, fitness for a particular purpose. The Publisher and Editor shall not be liable whatsoever for any errors, omissions, whether such errors or omissions result from negligence, accident, or any other cause or claims for loss or damages of any kind, including without limitation, indirect or consequential loss or damage arising out of use, inability to use, or about the reliability, accuracy or sufficiency of the information contained in this book.

Made with ♥ on the Notion Press Platform

www.notionpress.com

Another petal placed on the Lotus Feet of the Mother Of The Universe...

Contents

CONTENTS

CONTENTS

CONTENTS

A Word from the Author

✷

I started writing poetry pretty much late in life. The output, always sporadic, appeared on websites like boloji.com and poemhunter.com. No proper backup was maintained.

Recently, some well-wishers suggested publishing my writings. That turned out to be a very tough job. Fortunately, I could retrieve most of my writings from the above two websites. In all, there are two hundred and five poems. The first one hundred have already been published under the title "The Ascent". This is the second volume of one hundred and five poems. There is no chronology here as this is a hasty compilation from websites.

The title of this compilation is poem 69 - 'My First Love Letter'.

Some of my fellow poets/well-wishers have kindly said a few words about my poetry. Their esteemed opinions are included here. I thank them all from the bottom of my heart.

Trillions of thanks to Mr. Peter Hume for an excellent and affectionate foreword. He saved my day at the end.

May I assure you, my readers, that I write only when tremendously inspired and have a compelling concept/message to convey.

Wish you all a good read. Cheers!

Madathil Rajendran Nair

Coimbatore

January 2025

Foreword

It was by sheer accident that I came to know of Madathil Rajendran Nair. I was visiting an Indian friend of mine, a medico, in San Francisco, and there was this poetry book "The Ascent – Poetry Of Madathil Rajendran Nair – Vol. 1" languishing on his coffee table. The fresh smell of it suggested that it had never been touched. I just casually picked and opened it.

I never anticipated I was to begin a spectacular sojourn through marvelous poesy. The very first poem of the book "Anaesthesia" had me riveted. It was exalted metaphysics pouring in through an ordinary hospital experience.

I enquired who this poet was. My friend had no clue. He had received the book through a workmate, another doctor. I borrowed the book. My friend said I could keep it for good!

In the car, on my way back to Los Angeles, I devoured more than three-fourths of the one hundred poems of the book. Thank God, my brother-in-law was driving, and he was evidently peeved with my silent preoccupation with poetry.

That is just for an introduction. Now let me delve into matters more pertinent.

Upon further researches on the poet, I chanced upon a marvelous, long review of the book by an established Indian author and academician. I can't help quoting him…. "Nair is a poet of actualities but also loves depiction of disconnected life with an arcane technique. He rarely moves out of the region of realities and when he grasps vagueness, enigmas and ambiguity around, he is awesome in the sharpness of his linguistics arsenal."… WOW! I agree with folded hands. He can't be more accurate!

Having read the book in full, an urge arose in me to get in touch with the poet. That was strange – the poetry had me moved. Thankfully, there was a rubber stamp on the first page of the book with the author's Indian address, telephone number and email id. I sent him an email mentioning how much I was impressed. Pat came a reply of thanks saying he was around in the US at his daughter's residence in Dublin, Ca. She too is a doctor. I realized this world was indeed too small!

On a subsequent visit to San Francisco, I managed a one-hour rendezvous with the poet *en route* at Dublin. I found a simple man in simple attire – nearing octogenarian status in a couple of years. He was quite apart from the usual mundane hullabaloo. Despite significant hearing loss, he vibed with me well narrating how he trod into the realm of poetry after age sixty. His philosophical wisdom and its simple clarity astounded me. I left him with a request to write his thoughts on the philosophy of the East. He agreed, saying that he indeed was planning one.

He was immediately preoccupied with the publication of his second volume of one hundred poems – "My First Love Letter – Poetry Of Madathil Rajendran Nair – Vol. 2" (this book) and he hoped to publish it in January 2025 immediately upon his return to India. He followed up by sending a pdf of the proposed publication.

Now, just the day before, I received an urgent SOS from him if I could pen an introduction for the new book. Two of his contacts who had agreed to that task previously now have gone back on their commitment for reasons not known.

Writing intros isn't a job I am accustomed to. I was, therefore, initially reluctant. However, I have always loved poetry of the good old genre unaffected by the current, abstruse experimental maneuvers and complications. I knew that was the reason I liked Nair's writing. Moreover, his second volume was as good as the first one. Why not then take a plunge?

There was another reason I liked Nair. Like me, he was a chemistry student. However, he ended up in public relations in Kuwait. I write free-lance. He is into poetry. That is the only difference.

I therefore readily agreed to send him this note of appreciation. You may call it an intro or foreword – it doesn't matter.

Nair's poetry embraces philosophy, patriotism, humor, love for nature, and romance. The poem 'My First Love Letter' at # 69 is the title of the book. It is a phenomenal work that begins with adolescent infatuation and ends with a sigh of philosophical wisdom.

The poet, who seems to have spent some time in Arizona, marvels at the beauty of the mounts of Tucson and Sedona. Nature mesmerizes the reader through his Arizona poems. They too have abundant philosophy hidden in them. There is a very beautiful short one on Lord Ganesha of Maricopa. It is a gem. Towards the end of the book, we notice that Hawaii has also enchanted the poet and lent him enough material to wax philosophical.

'End Of The World' and 'Body And The Universe' at # 61 and 62 are philosophically mind-boggling. Rest assured, there are other poems of the same genre also packed in the book.

Nair has a piece on Narendra Modi, the current Indian Prime Minister. I know many who consider Modi a racist. But Nair hopes Modi's ascension to power to augur an era of equality in India without a minority-majority division. Having seen the PM's performance so far, and from what I hear from my Indian friends, I have reason to believe Nair is right in his expectations. All the best for his nation. There are a few other writes in the book that ooze patriotic fervor. Nair's love for his country is unmistakable.

Besides Modi, we have his exact opposite Che Guevara also extolled in one of the poems! Nair says Che continues to be the heartthrob and icon of the youth of Kerala, Nair's native State in India, despite the fact that he has been very much decried and exposed in recent days. Whatever, the poem is touching and a treat to read.

'Viewing The Album' at # 29 and 'Newspaper And A Broken Back' at # 39 are brilliantly rib-tickling. There are flashes of humor scattered elsewhere in the writings.

It is not possible to dwell upon each poem of the long list of one hundred and five. But believe me, all of them are good read and a large number of them just superb. For instance, 'Ode to Tsunami', 'Mumbai', 'Incredible India', 'Indian Motherhood', etc.

The book is old English poetry nostalgia condensed. It is a welcome relief in our current circumstances of rash poetic experimentation that taxes the brain. Nair says he writes free verse. However, there is a natural measure and rhythm in his writing suggestive of a hidden meter.

I consider myself lucky to have come across such a poet. While wishing him all success, I request poetry lovers across the globe to give him a big pat of encouragement.

Peter Hume

Freelancer

Los Angeles

January 24, 2025

What Poets and Friends Have to Say:

Mr. Nair has great flair for language and innate yen for lyricism. His poems capture reader attention with their free flow and vivid and picturesque portrayal. As a fellow poet, I have been an avid reader of his poems.

The most outstanding quality of his poems is the lofty diction and erudite style with not many on par. As effusions of a highly imaginative mind, they testify in ample measure to the transfiguring power of poetic fancy which raises the subject from its dull bed and lets it soar high on invisible wings. His poetic oeuvre captures elusive images in alluring metaphors. His poems will definitely strike a responsive chord in the hearts of the readers with the life lessons they impart, the sense of humour they obliquely give, the 'thumbnail' sketches of individuals he has met, the pen portraits of great personalities he admires etc. Some of his poems are pregnant with romantic overtones with imagery and passion in a symphony of words. While some poems are filled with love's timeless beauty and depth, some are highly devotional highlighting the need to commune with the inner power abiding within.

Above all, he is a bilingual poet and publishes poems in Malayalam - his mother tongue. His translations of works of poets of great renown to Malayalam are worth immense approbation. His ability to translate poems without marring their original beauty or sense is amazing and awe-inspiring.

Mr. Nair has displayed enormous linguistic skill in weaving words and imagery to create a collection of about two hundred outstanding poems and I am sure readers will receive his work with great warmth.

Wish the poet all success!

Valsa George

Poet

Retired Professor of English, Nirmala College

Muvattupuzha, Kerala

****

Madathil Rajendran Nair is an Indian poet of high stature who writes both in English and Malayalam with equal linguistic dexterity. His poems are like different coloured flowers, each having a distinct fragrance. They bear his signature of profound authority over English language and beauty in smooth flow of words, stirring the reader's heart with sweet emotions.

Mr.Nair's poems have great depth and insight and touch on a wide range of topics like love, nature, philosophy, social issues, historical facts and portraits of great personalities. His word-paintings are so beautiful that they leave an indelible impression on the minds of the readers.

Mr.Nair's portrayal of characters is superb with vivid imagery and chosen words that paint a perfect picture of the character and the reader is drawn into it as if he is seeing the characters himself.

In a nutshell, I shall say that the readers will find in his book a treasure of wonderful poems suffused with beauty, philosophy, wisdom and love, woven in a tapestry of beautiful words.

Bharati Nayak, Bilingual (English and Odia) poet, Writer, Translator and Editor,

Bhubaneswar, India.

****

I have several years of association with Mr. Madathil Rajendran Nair. He was in Kuwait Oil Company's Public Relations Group headed by me. He had always made sure that he mailed his writings to me first. For years, I kept encouraging him to publish his poetry in book form and not keep the beautiful words hostage in his notebooks. We deserve to enjoy them as well. That was in the early 2000s. I am therefore surprised why it took him so long, over twenty years, to take the publishing plunge.

Mr. Nair is a brilliant writer of depth.   His riveting poems centre mainly around nature and the philosophy of the East. He invariably makes sure that he conveys good and effective messages through his writings. His writings also show tremendous humour, romanticism and above all patriotism. I will enjoy reading his poems now that they are going to be out in one place!

I wish him all the best.

Abdul Khaleq Al-Ali

A friend

(Madathil asked me to write my work title, but I could not find a better word than FRIEND!)

Kuwait

****

Madathil Rajendran Nair's poetry compels the reader to ponder and reflect on relationships, family values, social anxieties, India's culture and its heritage, eulogies and psychological and philosophical topics. The two-part anthologies are a good and healthy read as they help to discover for oneself the moods and diversity of life.

Poet Rajender Krishan

New York

(Founder/Editor boloji.com)

****

Sir Madathil is a poet with deep insight and vast vision. Reading his poems makes me think that life is truly a learning experience. His poems are full of wisdom and his philosophical bent of mind is reflected in his poetry. His descriptive and narrative skills are wonderful. Most of all, his poems are significant and relevant to the world. I always enjoy reading his poems. An Inspiring writer of high stature.

Nosheen Irfan

A poet from Pakistan

@ poemhunter.com

****

Madathil Rajendran Nair started posting his poems at PoemHunter since 2014 and has already established his stamp. His poems have an inherent beauty and every line has enormous power since he chooses and arranges words with great care and thought. The topics of his poems range from philosophy, nature, current events, historical facts and so on. Whatever the topic he chooses, his clear understanding and his vast knowledge and experience trickle through. His past poems are finding their way out to be shared by others. I look forward to more and more poems from Madathil Nair to enrich the wonderful world of poetry.

Tirupathi Chandruapatla

A fellow poet

@poemhunter.com

****

1. It Rained Heavily in Tucson

It rained last night
Heavily in Tucson
The Rillito was in spate
Her gait was muddy
Like a temptress
Who had a nightlong orgy

I sat beside her
Watching her body sparkle
In demoniac frenzy
Moon-struck inebriate to the hilt

And then when I raised
My eyes to look
At the Catalina mounts
I found the image of a lady
Like in Victorian paintings
Holding her gown rushing
How sad we look at NASA images of Mars
Conjecture impossibilities!

And then beside her I did see
Hanuman-ji of one of my epics
Rushing past with a mount
On his left hand
To raise the ones who are dead

Imagery, alas, is subjective
And universal at the same time
Who pauses to nod in agreement
Only a very few
Who can transcend
Territorial fancies
And they are the hope
The world has to depend

It was a forenoon
When Victorian England
And ancient India
Converged to drink in
A moment of unparalleled beauty
On a land continents apart

I was the agency
I was happy
A jet passed by
In the skies
Perhaps from Phoenix
Leaving a silver trail
God knows who sat inside it
And if they shared my vision of beauty

No matter whatever
Those who carry
Beauty in their hearts
Will triumph forever

* 18 *

Tucson had night-long rain
Last night
She has swelled
To take in the whole universe
With me sitting
Beside her bowels
Muddy or whatever
In spate the Rillito river!

2. Rootless in a Vase

*[Inspired by "Flowers In A Vase" by Bulgarian Poet Alexander Shurbanov
(Translated into English by Ludmila G Popova-Wightman)]*

A bunch of rootless flowers
Stacked pleasingly in a vase
Hiding their pain, all in smiles
Placed on desktop
Just for our comfort

Like the rootless that roam the earth
Paining our sobbing conscience!
Is it not the same ache we have
Deep at the bottom of the heart?

Every human babe - is it not
A flower inside a vase
To pine, pine and pine
Looking at the forlorn star
Rootless on the plane called life?

3. Tucson the Ma Nonpareil

Betwixt a crimson west of sunset
Rainbow-crowned thunder cloud on the east
Swept by ferocious gales
Lay Tucson waiting
Her locks scattered
Her feet on the north
On the Catalina mounts
Head pillowed on Santa Rita
Voluptuous, for her mate, the sky to descend

As mesquites, palo verdes, oaks, figs, acacia
Waved their heads in demoniac dance
Lighted by an unearthly shine
As though possessed by the elements
An evening was about to gasp its last

And then it came in a clatter
The sky with fingers of rain
Stoked her insanity as she giggled
In puddles and streams
As the Rillito swelled in orgasmic passion
Oh, what a beautiful night it was to begin!

And what happened then
To the luminescent fig beetles
Delicate dragon flies
Arizona sister butterflies
That throng the sunny days
Of Tucson's breeze and glitter?

Don't ask stupid mind
She is a mother, she knows
She had them hidden safe
Under her locks
As the sky stoked and stoked
And as she giggled without end
That beautiful rainy night
Tucson, the ma nonpareil!

4. Unidentified Flying Objects

Come again, come again
Outside my window
As dome-shaped saucers
Shining an ethereal light

And, as I rush outside
In curiosity, play hide and seek
Fly over the trees
Vanish into the sky
In the starry expanse
The Milky Way girdles

UFOs! Ever remain unidentified
So that poetry we can weave
Yarns of mystery around you
Move about like somnambulists
Eyes raised and riveted in the skies
Anxious to capture your unpredictable flights

Sorry, some of us have been prosaic

Linked you to our nuclear sites

Made movies of aliens who maul and kill

Scamper like big roaches

Walk like encephalitis

Men in black

Conspiring with Heads of States

Dissect abductees

Like we do with mice

Humanity, it seems, is all set

For a paradigm shift

To assimilate a gruesome probability

In through the fringes of expanding reality

The mightiest State on the globe

Is dying to be abducted into it

The rest of the world then has no choice

Star-wars, death, destruction and pain

A sad repeat of past history

On extra-terrestrial scale.

If that is the shape of human wont

Of what avail impotent Gods could be?

UFOs! Please, therefore, ever remain
Unidentified stuff, for our fancy
To weave stories and mysteries
In boundless poesy
May we remain ever bound
To terrestrial territory
And may our eyes alone wander
The endless blue, and starry nights
For your desultory darts from eternity

Peace, Peace, Peace.

5. Baby Shower

Amidst decorations sat
The expectant mother
Her teeth gleamed in a jasmine smile
As guests and greetings poured in

She had her hand on her belly
The balloons around envied
It is a boy, the doc has said
A future footballer perhaps – he kicks

The baby shower went on
With music, dance and fun
An evening went crimson
With birds chirping in unison

As mom and dad rejoiced
Brooding the baby reposed
Head down, eyelids closed
His whole being verily light condensed

A light that would soon blossom
Into a world of many
Follow a karmic design
On creator's great fabric

* 26 *

Wish him well guests
May all that he sees
Be auspicious and may he
Walk an earth that is paradise
Strewn with flowers and silk

Peace, Peace, Peace!

6. Mumbai

(This poem was written in December 2008 immediately after the 26/11 terror attack on Mumbai.)

Mumbai lies bleeding again,
Ah me, she has been struck
By men of satanic design,
Senseless scary spectres,
In a horrible dance of terror.

She had seen her children die
In riots, blasts and fire,
They are again mowed down
Now in a nightmare
By wickedness unparalleled,
Devilish and devious.

Beautiful, bejewelled and demure
She made it always sure
That her children never had to suffer
And that they laughed aloud
Through summer, rain and cold,
Whether they huddled in huts,
Slept on littered pavements,
Were stacked like sardines
In streaking trains, clad in sweat,
Or ensconced in comfort
On Malabar, Pali, Cumbala Hills.

Her lap was home
For all those who came
From distant lands
Indian and abroad,
She was home for the persecuted
From all over the globe,
A cultured madam to the sailors,
Who set foot on her shores,
In their quest for gold and scents,
Gems, wisdom and condiments.

Her children were of diverse hue
Like a bird's colorful plume,
Like a rainbow on Arabian Sea
In the glitter of monsoon eve.

In you were blended, dear Mumbai,
Passion, culture, spice of life,
Hidden beneath your wealth and posh
Indeed was an unseen bond
That tied us rich and poor
All alike like gleaming gems
In a necklace of Indianness,
A marvel as ancient as Ganges
And our sacred unwritten scriptures.

We walked your streets
Like in a dream
As do romantic leads
In fairy-tales feathery light
Played on our silver-screens.
Our goals were sure,
Our eyes azure,
We never had time for care,
Your embrace was so secure.

Temple, church and mosque we built
Together in one-nation spirit.
We didn't think even the least
Varied Gods in them we placed,
For something sacred from our past
Told us we were never apart.

We cackled like Diwali crackers
As we feasted Ramadan nights,
We smiled like Christmas morn,
We were always one and one.

Alas, gone are those golden days
Of trust, friendship, healthy sport.
Ours now is a miserable lot
Full of distrust, venomous thought.

Laughter and felicity we forgot,
Distraught we are by the thought:
'The man next doors has a scheming look,
Looks askance, he's a crook,
Oh God, he has a different God,
Time now I preserved mine dear Lord'.

We lost our sleep, we lost our mirth,
We lost our soul of Indianness,
We built walls and barbed their tops
Mounting on them barking guns.

Indians died and in their place,
Hindus, Muslims, Christians rose,
Language split our souls apart,
For sons of the soil we all fought.

Down we sank - a diseased nation
Fertile ground for contagion.
Misguided religion, death and terror,
Our enemies have them without any measure.

They are indeed a vilely lot,
Who place bombs in market hearts,
Desecrate all our holy hearths,
Shoot and kill us sans any thought.

Drunk of political power, drained of wit,
Leaders of the masses wilt,
Cringing for crumbs, alms and favor
On long corridors of power,
Puppets moved by perpetrators
Of crimes, arson, riots, who conspire
To undermine what remains
Of our humane Indianness
And our strides in sciences
All the way up to the Moon's surface.

Impotent we stand and witness
The gruesome terror senseless,
A volcanic rage fumes inside
As poor Mumbai bleeds and wails
Her sons fall in acts of bravery
Never heard before in history
Sanguine buds in a sacrificial pit
In the darkness of November nights.

A nation cries aloud to heavens
To send her a savior son,
Alas! in the pitch darkness around
Will she ever find that dear one?

Will her prayers ever be heard?
Will he come half-clad,
With a disarming smile, bespectacled,
Holding a walking stick, of concrete will,
Speaking a language of peace?
Or will he be seen under a tree
With a message to set us free
In the Kingdom of our Indianness
Of Love's Universal Consciousness?
Peace, Peace, Peace.

7. Avul Pakir Jainulabdeen Abdul Kalam

Kalam is no more
A sage has passed away
A saint of action who lived his words
A human god who trod among human forms

Grace descended upon us from the heavens
When the usually warring politicians
Like a flash in a pan
Chose an angel to adorn
The tallest chair of the nation

Kalam, forgive my calling you so
Without the usual titles of respect
Because you were so very much with us
Unlike most heads of states
And moved among us as simple
As an amused kid in a park
A smile always perched on its face

You were truly Grace personified
And rode political storms
Misrepresented religions
Intrigues and machinations
Remained aloof and untouched
Like a lotus leaf in a murky pond
Keeping always the good of the nation in mind

That was a great feat
For a great writer and architect
Of a nation's nuclear, defence and space dreams
To escape getting enmeshed
In the trappings of luring power

The nation should have made you
Its president for life
But, alas, that was not to be
Opportunism and political chicanery
Can't afford angels in office
When hell is what they design

Kalam, you proved unique and exemplary
Raised the status of your august office to the skies
In a manner even your esteemed
Predecessors would have envied

You have now flown away
Flapping your wings
Like the eagle of one of your sayings
Above the clouds
Untouched by the rains

Indians one and a quarter billion

Prostrate here under a darkening sky

Beseech you: "Kalam, come back again

Help us show the world

What being secular means

Breaking an atom for peace

Being the king and yet remain a kid

A love-soaked human to the hilt

That even gods would envy"

8. Incredible India

(This poem was written on 3rd November 2013 on the occasion of Diwali festival when the mood in India was upbeat with a cricket victory over Australia, the mainstay of which was Rohit Sharma's double-century.)

Boom, boom

The whole country blooms

It is Diwali time

The festival of colourful lights

Hail the Mother

Who vanquished

Devious demons of evil design

A rich country

Of poor people

As an old leader said

Past one and a quarter billion

Rejoices in sheer abandon

Deep into the night

Blazing their skies

With rockets

That flash, thunder and rain

Sparkles of every hue

That can be imagined

The firepower of the show
Ingenuity of its design
And the money that is burnt
Can perhaps put man on the stars

Everyone of every creed
And every faith
The poor as well as the rich
Forget differences
At least for once
And revels sans any reins

Luck this time
Has brought them a bonus
As Rohit lighted
The Bangalore skies
With his double ton of sixes
To vanquish the Aussies
In cricket
In a legend rewrite

The Gods have found the show
So irresistible
They enter the stage
Charioting
North East Monsoon clouds
With thunder claps
And brilliant bolts

It is past midnight
The carnival has to end
Those celebrating victory
Of the Mother
Or their cricket team
Have to return to their beds
Stomachs overstuffed or inebriate
To snore the rest of the night
Right up to the morrow's noon

But a frail old mother
Who loves her kids
Yet ravaged
By their whims and sins
Will stay awake
Worrying how she could
Herd them together
Put the house in order

And then in the wee hours
Before Venus calls
She will move towards
The Holy Ganges
Across the rocks
Against the winds
For her sacred bath

Dragging her failing frame
Gasping for breath
Supported by her tricolor staff
She will look at the stars
And pray for her sleeping calves

And that is Mother India
Oh, sleeping ignorant ones
Who of you would be there then
Awake and alert to give Her a hand
Say "Am with you mom"
And help Her embrace
The folds of Mother Ganges
For a holy dip of resurgence

To that one only India and Diwali belong
That one alone is heir supreme
To the Incredible India of our dreams

9. White Rock

In the middle of nowhere
On the new national highway
Transfixed I stood
With a broken-down car
An April sun fumed above

I had just passed a board
Which named the place White Rock
There wasn't anything white around
Just a small village of scattered huts
Looming black granite hills
Surrounded by desultory woods

Perhaps a pearly rock hill white
Had stood there before
An extreme singularity
And unwillingly given way
To the tapering highway
A geological marvel
A prehistoric volcanic spit
Or a meteor that landed with a fiery thud

No one knows
And in moonlit nights
It might have resembled from above
A domed UFO hidden in the woods
Lovers of the village had sat on it
Shared their sweet aches in tight embrace

Or in the morning sun
Cobras had mated at its foot
Their moist mouths in rainbow hue
Hooded bodies coiled like vine
In sublime dance of ecstasy

It has vanished without a trace
A keyhole to prehistoric past
The Sun sprang illusory pools
On the unending asphalt tape
That fumed and ran further down
Into an unknown future
Christened a nation's dream
Sans any link to the past

10. The Lord of Maricopa

In the wilderness of Arizona
Overlooked by mountains from the West
Devotees have Lord Ganesha housed
At the heart of Maricopa
In a temple that spires
Into the blue skies
And competes
With the mounts of Sierra Estrellas

The Lord is roused every morn
By the moos of cattle
From farms that abound
In the surrounds
Winds of the Sonoran desert pay obeisance
With the abundant aroma
Of peas, pecans, melons, citrus and alfalfa

I ventured into His presence
In the early morning breeze
Charged with the scent of incense
Flowers, camphor and turmeric

Smiling sat the Lord of elephant visage
Granting boons to one and all
The great remover of obstacles
In a desert town that once had
Received and sent dreamers in hordes
Into the arms of wilderness
In quest of gold to the North
As trains through day and night
Screeched and rattled on adamant tracks

Outside the door on my way back
A brownie dog stood guard
His face, I thought, spoke of a Mexican past
Whom I befriended with the biscuits I had
Into a playful bonhomie that sang
The world is one and the Lord too so
May all we see be auspicious too
The Lord inside sure did smile

11. Punching Bag

It hung in a corner of the living room
The worn-out punching bag
Wrinkled all over its leathery shine
Shuddering every time someone opened the door

My first daughter entered first
Contempt burning in her eyes
Punched the bag left and right
Like boxer Muhammad Ali
Making it swing violently
Hit the walls on either side

A few minutes afterwards
The second one had her turn
She came in dancing
Furiously punched panting
Turned her back to the bag
And then gave it a donkey kick

'Ere the poor bag could regain
Peace and equipoise
There entered my wife
Like a tempest unleashed
Danced and jumped around
Punching, panting, cursing
And then let out a scream
Like the famous "kreegaah"
Of ape-man Tarzan-ji

All three had their reasons:
An affair not receiving
Parental approval and blessing
A college excursion missed
Due to need for spending less
An unbought diamond ring
On wedding anniversary

Hung upside down
Was me - the real punching bag
In the middle of feminine power
Paunch sagging like the chin
Of Droopy of the cartoons
Receiving volleys of punches
Hitting the walls relentlessly

12. Endless Tragedy

There was a grand-father tamarind tree
In front of my ancestral home
Pointing a bare finger into the sky

In the grey of monsoon drizzle
Early in the morning
A brooding crow which had a hole in one of its wings
Used to perch on it

That was my pre-teen childhood
When I had two aunts
With two cows – one white and the other grey
Whose calves were my constant companions
As I wandered in surrounding woods
Watching birds laboring at their nests

We had kerosene lamps then
Under which I used to mug up lessons
When I looked askance at the sky
The orange Arcturus
Winked at me from Bootes
Leaves giggled in the wind

My dad took his pompous strolls
In the sprawling courtyard
Watching if I misbehaved
As mom garnished
Chutney for breakfast
Spreading dosas on the pan

Those were beautiful days
Which I took for granted
Would ever remain
Unchanged through to endless time

But, alas, as time sped
As I witnessed my body change
Through teenage to adulthood
Each of the things I loved
Vanished one after another

Mom and dad were washed away
In the tides of time
So were the aunts
Someone axed the tamarind tree
The crow made homeless perished
The cows and calves too disappeared
Into the hungry bowels of abattoirs

The house was sold
New ones displaced the woods
As I fled to distant lands
A wandering nestless bird
Ever on restless wings

Aging all the time
Into an insipid mass
Of failing musculature
Through pain and fatigue
Into the grey and wrinkles
Of a geriatric mess

When the wick of knowing fades
In slumber's chamber every night
The mess does wonder
What is it that has remained
Unchanged watching the river of time
Displace the known with unknown things
Wash a body into bones and skin

Yet, the mess languishes in mess
Never ever able to accept
That it really is the witness
The changeless awareness
That remains ever untouched
Lo, my tragedy is thus abetted

13. The Man Who Cannot Retire

He danced and waved in the drizzle and wind
The man who can't retire
Headlights shone on him
Like bulging eyes of the night
Lengthened the comic shadow of his royal turban
Onto the woods and yonder into the far beyond
The man who once guarded a nation's frontiers

Outside a restaurant, on the thorny fringe of the road
In the chill, his knees and heels misbehaved
Like obstinate kids who refuse to be roused
Out of slumber, unable to open laden eyes

Seventy years of privations weighed
His steps were stiff and rigid
But dance and wave at passers by
He had to, that is the boss's bidding
The owner of the restaurant
Who had his eyes in the stars
And dreamed of eternal stampede
At his grand portal on the road

An ailing wife, two daughters
Abandoned by their reckless men
Their screaming kids had to be fed
The dancer couldn't simply retire
The man who once guarded a nation's frontiers

The boss had said
He could have hired
Pretty lasses for the work
But in a land of predators
And foraging cannibals
He couldn't place them on the road
To bring in prospective customers
Men retired from service
Was therefore the right choice

So dance like them the hired hand must
If he wished to keep his bread
No matter how old he was
Even if his feet were bare
And badly tattered his royal attire

The dancer wished he could pause
Move into the shadow of the gate
Ease his stiffening gait
Light a beedi, puff at it
Look at the stars that rode the trees

But who knows there isn't

A cop lurking in the dark

Engaged in overkill

On smoking ban for a petty bribe

And then there always is

The boss with a thousand eyes

From anywhere any time he can spot

Any dereliction on the part of his staff

Old days were perhaps good

In the trenches on the frontiers

When the rum in the vein

Ruled men's actions

When panic moved triggers

The stink of sweat and boot

Didn't matter

And which way death came

A bullet, a shrapnel or grenade

Or perhaps an unseen bayonet from behind

When deep in the trench he lay

With other soldiers over-frayed

His wife and kids a memory half-erased

Like the moon of the day

Looking at the winter sky

Thinking why men fought and killed

Over disputes on geographical lines

On a planet that belonged to none

He knew perhaps there were men
Like him in trenches across the line
Who thought on similar lines
Wished to stand up and embrace
Throwing their guns to winds

But that was not to be
For fear was the key
Any movement across the line
Be that the wriggle of a roach
The finger on the trigger should broach

Fear is the key, yes, fear is the key
His bread, come what may, he must keep
Dance he should till his feet did bleed
In the rain, chill and wind
The pathos should ensure
Footfalls in the restaurant
The man who can't retire
The man who once guarded a nation's frontiers

14. Haiku Comments

(These are some of my comments on the haikus of other fellow poets slightly altered where needed in order to let them stand alone.)

Cloud:

The cloud is in haste
It has to rain on the plains
Hot thirsty terrains

Peepholes:

Questions start with why
When, what and how – they all are
Peepholes that describe

In Orbit:

I remain unsent
Due to your gravity's pull
Planet in orbit

Reality Of Life:

I don't want to leave
But leave I must that is life
Sunshine, there is cloud

Carbon:

We are made of dust
Carbon therefore suits us best
Silicon can hurt

Pain:

Forgetful we are
Court pain again and again
'Coz of ignorance

Tequila:

With salt on glass brim
Tequila is simply great
Hell with the liver

Sensitive Throats:

Even with hot drinks
Ice is pretty dangerous
Some sensitive throats

Water:

Two gases combine
A magic liquid is born
Blossoms of life bloom

Bread:

The bread is pretty
Send me a loaf fast pretty
Taste-buds are greedy

Ladybug (not a haiku) :

But why are they called bugs
When enchant is all they do
Unlike bugs and the lady of the house
Who bug us without a cease?

Poet (not a haiku) :

Tell me of what ethereal wine you are drunk
That so much poesy brims in your head
Like glowing glow-worms without a cease
Casting imagery day and night?

15. Indian Housewife

With the batter
And the ladle
On the pan
She drew a picture
As her toes did do
On the floor
A dream unknown
Humming a Tamil song

Her sweat longed
For her man
Yet to return from work
As the evening collapsed
Into uneven darkness
That knew no heart

Pancakes and pancakes
Made she with vengeance
Stacked them on plate
And waited for her man

He came all sweat
Inebriate to hilt
Went to bed
Snored and bored the night
She wept beside

The Indian housewife
Who drew her dreams
On silly pans
That fried dosas
And cried all night

Wind and cloud
Do you mind
Giving her company
This hapless night?

16. Ecological Doom

Research says
The funeral pyres
Across our land
Cause global warming
Himalayan snow to melt
As do the fires lit
At religious rituals and worship

Beware therefore
Before you light
Incense before the Gods
The Diwali lamps
Not to mention the crackers

Scientists whose moustache hair
Is yet to attain the natural sheen
Of adulthood
Funded by international aid
Are doling out
New gospels for the world to follow

Beware and shudder
Cast your ancient wisdom
Away and embrace
The new vision of science
That predicts
Ecological doom
Every second of the day

Forget your forefathers
Who brought in the rains
By lighting ritual fires
Laid down rules
To celebrate your festivals
At the peak of summer
With fireworks
In order to seed the clouds
And gave you the best way
To dispose of the dead

Ecological doom
Ecological doom
Caused by funeral fires!
When your modern factories
Are sending
Many hapless ones
Early to their unfortunate pyres!

Exaggeration is our wont
Sensationalism our forte
The media is playing court
With vested interests no doubt

And there is this crow
Who gives me company
When I sip my morning tea
On whose wisdom I rely

There are crows and crows
Birds and birds
But we rarely see
Any one of them lying dead
I asked my friend what they did
With the cadavers of their friends

He cocked his head
And cawed out aloud
Ask your scientists
To eat the dead

Wise guy he is
Our scientists now
Should follow his advice
And sit down to eat
Their sumptuous meals
Aproned well
With fork and knife

17. The Buddha and Happiness

Your idol sits calm in my living room
I pass by it at least a hundred times
But never have time even to notice it once
How am I then to pause and listen
To your ancient message of wisdom
The panacea for universal peace?

Your image is just a decorative piece
That boasts of my spiritual side
When I really am miserable
Driven by innumerable wants
In a crazy samsara that ceaselessly haunts

I keep running helter-skelter
In search of the fruition of my desires
And happiness, always out of reach
Receding into the horizons
Mirages the chase of which
Gives only fatigue and pain in the end

You had the courage to renounce
All that you thought belonged to you
And wander about seeking truth
Till it revealed in blazing clarity
In the sprawling shade of a Bodhi tree

Please tell me how that will came about
And will it be mine if I beseech
You everywhere, every second, without cease
So that without a trace of guilt
I can rescind all my roles —
Husband, son and everything
Like you did that lonely night

Or, have I got it all very wrong?
A story goes that someone said
"It is happiness that I want"
And you asked him with a smile
To get rid of the "I" and "want"

What then remained was "happiness"
Sure that was what you really meant
The seeker himself is happiness
If he stopped being the seeking self

Please grant me, therefore, the will

To leave my wants and ego at Your Feet

Please put me under a Bodhi tree

So that I can play my roles

Whatever they are as come by

Like a Buddha, enlightened, serene

Unhaunted by world's trappings

As a piece of happiness that is peace

18. Miracle Cure

He was unconventional
Swam against the tides
A village man of medicine
Rock-firm in his methods

And he did isolate a plant extract
That restored the pancreas
Effected miracle cure
Of diabetes one and two once for all

Success embraced him because
He didn't buy the age-old edict
That sugar disease once in
Can never be reversed

As he rejoiced over his discovery
Pharmaceutical chiefs drowned in worry
In the world's mega-cities
Which headquartered the industry

They spent sleepless nights
The new drug would make obsolete
Their formulation armouries
Of costly hypoglycaemics

Perennial springs of wealth
Scattered all over the world
That sucked into the pockets
Of rich and poor regardless

And that would mean losses in tons
Running into billions, nay trillions
All due to a new panacea
Hit upon by a hardened Hippocrates

Telephones rang at several spots
All over the globe late into night
When at last the morning dawned
The medic failed to rise and yawn

He was found sitting in his lab
His head bent over the desk
There was a public uproar
And a final autopsy report

A cardiac arrest it was
Following a massive attack
The doc who signed the report
Smiled his way to the bank

He too was truly baffled
How such a fine lethal needle
Found its way right to the heart
Leaving no external marks

19. Narendra Modi

(This poem was written in 2014 when Mr. Modi first rode the crest of a popular wave to power. I don't want to sit in judgment of his performance during the last ten years or listen to what his detractors have to say, as even they would admit that this gentleman is quite unlike an Indian in that he doesn't sit idle even for a second. This poem now is a hope against hope.)

A wistful nation prayed and yearned
And then, their summer dreams at last have flowered
Modi, please take the reins and lead
Grant them the deliverance they need

They didn't vote for a party or a group
They chose a man they sensed
Within themselves who would sure
Effect their post-independence sins a cure

And you happen to be the worthy son
Who called dear India mother
On a land where statesmen had scampered
Hither and thither hoping to 'discover' their mother!

And where politicians of every hue
Have cried victory to her aloud
While away from public eye
Worked for selfish ends in the sly

She is on her sick bed, gasping for breath
Kneel beside her, help her stand
And walk towards a brilliant morn
Across the great Gangetic plains

On to a land sans minorities
Or a majority, but of true equality
Of the fullness of our Indianness
Which one and a quarter billion equally share

Take us ahead Modi, we can't wait
Blessed are you, mom has her hand on your pate
Our roots are bleeding, no more wait
We don't care two hoots
For the balderdash your detractors mouth

20. Let Us Rouse Our Vegetating Psyche

(The sad news of Aruna Shabaugh's death headlined newspapers across India. She was a nurse at King Edward Memorial Hospital, Parel, Mumbai. She went into a vegetating coma after a ward-boy sexually assaulted her in 1973 and remained in that state at the same hospital for the last forty-two years under the care of her colleagues/staff. The hospital was just across the street from Haffkine Institute where I was working at the time of the incident. Although I am happy her ordeal has ended, the news of her passing away broke me down. A tsunami of empathy engulfs me and I wish the whole nation is washed by it.)

Aruna Shanbaugh has left

Forty-two years of vegetating has ended

On a King Edward Memorial Hospital bed

When uncaring time morphed a dreamy damsel

Into a wrinkled mass of grey sixty-eight without her knowledge

They said she had been conscious

But perhaps not aware

Of what was going on around her

Well, all that is a matter of conjecture

Now for fruitless debaters.

Who can understand a caged bird's frantic flaps

Behind the jail-bars of blocked senses?

I had worked just across the street

From where she was trespassed

Our ways might have crossed on the roads

Without our knowledge, we were strangers

As she then hadn't the tragic identity

Which calamity imposed on her with horrendous cruelty

As she lay looking blankly at the ceiling

In the care of her untiring colleagues

The law spent a lot of heartless time

Deciding the nature of the crime

Society debated if euthanasia was the need of the time

Forty-two dead years of national vegetating

During which millions of mothers and sisters

Across our land were brutally disrobed and shamed

An orgy that continues even now unabated

Despite our loud and empty claims

Aruna, how sad your tragedy hasn't taught the men

The lessons they should have learnt

Long, long ago, that a woman too is a friend

Not a piece of meat, and should be treated like an equal confidant!

Why have we failed in drilling this theme

Into the head of every male child of our land

Right from birth, so it pauses

Later in life to salute in respect

Whenever a woman crosses its route?

The granite stones of King Edward
Are tearful this morn of humid May
A bird that had housed in it
For a long while has just flapped away

Men of the nation, ask yourselves
If her plight has welled your eyes
And torn your hearts, if yes
Get to your feet, rouse this nation's psyche
From the vegetating coma it is in

May dear Aruna rest in peace
May her story never repeat

21. Remover of Obstacles

In every Tamil village or town
When a road can't go straight
And parts into the hands of a T
There presides an idol
Of the remover of obstacles
Lord Ganesh with elephant visage
Reverently placed

Day and night, rain or sun
Tempest, floods or deluge
He sits there smiling
Granting passers by
Apparent choice to choose left or right

Blessed are the ones
Whom he guides
Left or right
He is always right
They never rue
Have no worries
About paths trodden
No dilemmas about roads not taken

Such is the faith
The obstacle-remover grants
With Him therefore begins
All beginnings that are planned
At the T-junctions of life
There ain't then any culs de sac

22. Armed Rebellion

Cops, cops everywhere
Uniformed, disguised, armed
The dental clinic looked
A heavily guarded fort

The reason - a female Maoist
Languishing in police nest
Who with her husband believed
Armed rebellion is a must
To redeem the sorry lot
Of the poor and oppressed
Had a tooth that badly ached

The dentists were to see
How bad was the case
A single escort would have sufficed
But the cops had their worries
They gathered in full force
As though at a State parade
Lest a rescue attempt was made

The whole building was emptied
Patients rashly shooed
Away 'ere the celebrity arrived
Secure, ensconced, in the middle
Of cops male and female

A poor Municipal sweeper
Who scavenged the streets
Squatted watching the scene
Holding his aching chin

He hadn't slept the whole night
As hell had housed in his mouth
An armed rebellion of sorts
Of germs, pus and pain

He prayed for the celebrity to leave
Fast so he gets some relief
Who is there to know his pain
When armed rebellion rules the brains?

So he sat in the burning sun
With a bursting fire under his chin
A spider made homeless
An ant heavily crushed
In his own land of make-believe

23. Mother's Day

It was Mother's Day
I flew with a mom and her naughty boy
Over biscuity golden clouds
In American skies
From Houston to New York

My mother had her prime in an age
The Wright brothers flew dragon-flies
Sparrows with broken wings
Uncertain of their landings

The mother tended her child
Attending to his every need
Patient, composed, saintly, divine,
Never forgetting to place
Silent kisses on his rosy cheeks

I sat beside her and wept
The noisy child of yore
His hair and thoughts ruffled
Starry eyes distraught
Now caged in a distant past
Like that ubiquitous portrait
Of the crying boy
That adorns our modern walls
Oh mother, thou shalt live ever long!

24. Red Roses on the Nation's Feet

This morning
At a temple across my street
Drums thumped
A nation's heart-beats

And bells clanked
To rouse my Mother in slumber
A Nation sang
Its national anthem
With chins raised

Far away on a frontier land
More than forty sank
Sons, brothers, husbands
Those who killed them have no regard

Mercenaries of thought
Religion, mental contagion
Awaiting bliss in a heaven
Across vast lands of dark ignorance

Sanguine roses fell on the feet of the Nation
She can't be swayed
Aye, you wait perpetrators
Mother will have her last say

We will come back upon you
With all our ferocious might
This battle is ours
To win which we will spare no effort

Sure, you will flee in fright
No matter wherever you hide
Scoundrels, think aloud, don't you look like
Mad dogs barking on the streets?

Amen.
Oh, that is a call
We have no problem
Chanting it out aloud
For we have always been
Birds chirping peace
Aum, Aum and always Aum
Who is there to discern?

25. The Yamuna in Rage

(Written in December 2012 when Nirbhaya, the unfortunate gang-rape victim, was breathing her last on a Singapore hospital bed and public anger in New Delhi and elsewhere was at boiling point)

You have given me hope
My veiled and unveiled sisters
Muslim and Hindu
Belonging to every faith
Marching towards the historic India Gate
Defying the might
Of the overbearing insolent State

Demanding justice for women
Justice for Indian womanhood
Fighting death on a hospital bed
With its last insecure breath
A weak palpitating heart

You have taught me
India is one
It shall ever remain so
Forever for eons to come
Veiled or unveiled
No matter what faith inspires it

We have one common goal
Justice for the downtrodden
The unfortunate oppressed
And victimized
Irrespective of religion

Let your voice be heard
And reverberate
On the corridors of power
We have reached the Armageddon
The Kurukshetra of our times

Let the adamance
And insolence
Of the impudent power-brokers shudder
Let them take notice
No more foolery is allowed
And take to their trembling feet and flee

Let new blood flow
In your veins
Brothers and sisters
Like the beloved Yamuna in rage
Let us compose the tune
For a new India to sing
Vande Mataram again

In grand solemn salute
To oppressed Indian womanhood
All that is weak
And taken for granted
Callously trespassed

So that the weakening breaths
And ebbing pulse
Of Indian womanhood
On a distant hospital bed
Are not wasted
And washed away
In the waters of uncaring time
To indifferent oblivion

Let the Yamuna be in rage
Let the Yamuna be afire
Rise sisters and brothers
You have reached your Armageddon
At a New India Gate
Awaiting history to be made

26. Daily Eating (Haiku)

Break-fast they call it
Fast it was because I slept
Break-sleep it should be

It goes by the name
Lunch, even if you did brunch
Marks wasted day's waist

It is dinner time
Over-eating sure assures
A show of nightmares

27. Some Downpours

When monsoons from South West and North East
Deluge us for over half of every year
Why is it that only certain downpours
Stand out in memory etched
Carved out like sculptures?

There was the one that came late in the afternoon
Far from the east, the clouds cumulonimbus
Looked like an array of caparisoned pachyderms
They advanced trumpeting thunder claps
Plunging the world in darkness
Unleashed their fury and set rindles in spate

Then there was the one which poured the whole day
Unabated without wind or thunder but several inches
Drowning and washing away huts, men and animals
And capturing headlines on the papers of the morrow

There was that beautiful one
Which came when sleepless you rolled on the bed
As the night listened like an attentive mammoth
Its ears and eyes focused like an arrow into the yonder
First it was a distant murmur, the wind didn't whisper
Then an approaching roar over silent forests
Till the staccato began on the rooftop

Then again there was the midnight visitor
Least expected, materializing from nowhere
None, even the weatherman, could say where it originated
Windless, steady, pouring out for hours
With paced thunder and lightning as though preset
Pulling you out of your bed
On to the verandah to inhale
Its abundant aromatic spray
Where the moths would gather in glee
To perform around a silent kerosene lamp

Oh, such downpours are wonderful things
Praise be to the one who sends them
To fill our hearts with mirth
And etch unforgettable nostalgia in our memory

28. Sunset Haiku Trinity

Bleeding sun succumbs
No one sheds any tears
Assured of rebirth

Bird sees the sunset
Wonders where the fruit has gone
Uneaten orange

Sunset hour ending
West blushes like a damsel
Picks starry nightgown

29. Viewing the Album

My friend's daughter got married
And his wife invited my better half
To view the wedding album

A genius close to Bollywood
Had it in Mumbai designed
Aided by brilliant Bangalore techies
And the photos had cost my friend
Several hundred thousands

We had attended the wedding
And having witnessed the proceedings
I asked my wife what is there again
So much to see in a recording

She ruled I was asinine
With an unwed daughter in the house
I needed to familiarize
How the Joneses were conducting
Leaving me perspiring
At the thought of outdoing
My friend's wanton squandering

Choiceless I dogged
Her to my friend's abode
On the way she warned
I was rather clumsy
Needed to be interactive
With society than rot like a rustic

She instructed me to wow
Never ever yawn
Throughout the gruesome viewing
The hosts would be keen
About our comments and reactions
We shouldn't disenchant
The good heavenly souls

Yes, they were indeed keen
Of angelic countenance
I could see them askance
Looking at our faces
Rejoicing at our pretense

And I was horrified
There were in all five
Fat albums in a line
We would certainly age
Before we viewed the whole footage

I wowed at every snapshot
Like an exultant school brat
Perhaps, the act I overdid
The pain in my wife's friendly nudges said

The hosts poured over us
Explaining who was who
When, where and how
Things that didn't matter
To be forgotten sooner than later

The maid brought some tea
I just cursed my friend
I had expected drinks
To pep up my morale
Through that tiring ordeal

I sipped half the tea
Left half in the cup
My mom had taught
People of gentle breed
Never gulped or devoured
The whole of what was offered
A tip my wife also approved

We viewed the albums
Late past dinner time
My back was giving in
When the last page was seen

Thanking God I placed
The last album on the board
God wasn't that kind
The half-full cup toppled

Out into an uncertain night
Back home I followed a muttering wife
With a clumsy gait daring not
To look at her glaring eyes

30. Our Ignorance

(Written when Bhagwan Satya Sai Baba passed away)

We wept, we prayed, we stood vigil
Pressed our heads against the grilled hospital gate
Hoping some movement inside
Would signal positive tidings

We called in the police
Lest something untoward happened
As fools discussed the money at stake
And your corporeal body lay inside
Breathing its last
Supported by ventilators
And intravenous stimulators

Baba, I had laughed at you
When you visited my village
In my young days
I dubbed your acts
Magical pranks
I was then atheistic
And morbidly rationalistic
Not knowing what
Being either really did mean
I could but only do
What every other rascal did

I grew up enough
Perhaps wise enough
To admit that the world
Couldn't exist at all
In the first place
Sans some intelligence
Which knew it
And homed in it
Like itself
No matter what name
We called it by

I could then resonate
With what you said
Yet doubts remained
But I could at least
Remain neutral and avoid
Being foolishly judgmental
Like the erstwhile young scoundrel

Now you have flown away
All things born have to fade away
The play of the last so many days
Has come to an end
Giving our ignorance a field day
Of speculation why
A saint was embodied
Suffered mortal tragedies

Disease, doctors, gadgets
And what not
A whole world of medicine
Every-hour bulletins
A frail failing body amidst
In the throes of entropy
That our blind eyes
Had for years
Sought for darshan
Not knowing what lay behind

We wept and wailed
Prayed for a miracle in vain
Refusing to open our eyes
To the truth of our being
That you are
For we always relished
Being mundane
Fastidiously inane
Accustomed to embodied gods
That strode our roads
Rubbing shoulders with us
No matter how much
You and others strived

Now, Alas! There is talk
Of a resurrection, reincarnation
Your promised return
To the darkness of our ignorance
To enact another play
For us to foolishly devour
With eyes that are blind
To the light that lights the stage

Groping in daylight is our incurable wont
Our backs eternally turned to the sun

Peace, Peace, Peace

31. Inebriation

Nostrils smell the air
Acrid, salty, ammoniac, thin
A world resides in odour
Like fumes of camphor
A sunset in wet hour

Inebriation they call it
Coming from the realm of spirits
Tipsy speech and gait
Courage volatile
Blurred image
Like a receding mirage

So be it, I don't care
As long as I walk
This labyrinthine life
Watching the fun
Laughing out aloud
Singing my hymns

And smelling all along
The tree, the dog, the alley cat
Murky carpet wet
Incense before my Gods
As the clouds pour
Over the peaks
Torn asunder
By bolt and thunder

Oh, life is a beautiful petal
Tossed by eternal winds
On an unending plain
We take it transitory -
An everlasting pleasure
Where bodies fall
And then new ones are found
Providential replacements
In a drunkard's endless dream.

32. Dust Winds

It is raining dust outside
But seems mysterious mist
Through the tinted glass
Of my office
In the Arabian Gulf
This oil-rich desert land
A man-made haven of comfort

It comes they say
From far off lands
Like Ethiopia
Where stomachs burn
In scorching famine
A waterless terrain
Blessed by the genesis
Of the extolled great Nile

And as I look listening
To the hum of the a.c.
My spine radiating bliss
Of make-believe grace
Hollows stare at me

Set in them are cat-eyes
In the dark of the night
Of fire, thirst and hunger
That shame and haunt
My hypocritical posture

The dust-winds blow unabated
Clouding my vision
Every condemned being's
Incurable blindness
An unceasing retribution

33. Netaji

A whole nation yearned
And still hopelessly yearns
For your return
An unrealistic dream
If human lifespan is any frame

We had many wishful rumours
You were alive somewhere
You will again return
On an auspicious morn
That marks victory of good over evil
To lead us in our hopeless struggle

Our walls adorned your visage
Bespectacled, untouched by age
The burning eyes under an upheld forehead
Setting afire our nationalistic pride

That you had vanished
Without leaving any trace
Stories of your heroic escapades
No doubt kept your legend green

That you didn't return to be sullied
Like other leaders who dirtied
Their repute by playing court
To the damsels of power and politics
Sustained your pristine purity

India is an inveterate nation
That believes in rebirth
Lifespans do not concern us
So your return has always been certain

Or you are already there
Tell me please
Which hut on this vast land of ours
Now cradles you, Netaji?
My ears are pining for your cry -
The war-cry - before my old frame caves in
For our shattered dreams to gather around
And whirl a twister all across the land

Please don't make this dream go vain
Wishful thinking again
Can't a whole nation's desire
Move huge mountains aside?

Return please to our side
In whatever form you decide
To an unlucky nation that is accustomed
To weave and cling to impossible dreams

34. M C P*

He placed his head on the idol's feet
In soulful prayer
For his wife and kids
The world and all that lived

Didn't the age-old prayer say
In pristine Sanskrit
"All that I see,
All the worlds, as worlds are the seen,
Be auspicious and happy"?

His better half, vociferous like Greer
Her fair body clad in chiffon
Like a lollypop in transparent wrap
Told her friend
I can't stand the guy
*My husband, he is an MCP**

He asks the kids to pray
Prescribes ancient texts
Picked from scriptures
That have lost their sway
Pries into what they read
Detests the TV they are glued

Her friend cackled
In effervescent bursts
"He sure is the last,
Don't care two hoots
If the first two are true"

Chiffon-pack chuckled
Like a cuckoo bird
To join in the mirth
The humour was worth
Loud mouthful laughter

Let us hurry to the club
Work still awaits
Before the evening meet
On the fight for our oppressed ilk

Let us clad ourselves well
A woman's success dwelled
In her body cleverly wrapped
Age didn't matter
And in the degree of discomfort
It gave young male rabbits
Who throng women's meets

Meanwhile, the pig toiled
Between his factories
His mind fully occupied
With how to plan taxes
Manage the kids' expenses
Pay their growing spectacle bills
Settle the wife's vagaries
And run an empire growing beyond his skills

The union guy demands
A new television
On top of a cell phone
Gifted a week before
The nasty guy must be laid to rest
Lest he steals peaceful sleep
Shouting proletarian rights

He recalled the way he began
From scratches on days bygone
In the city suburb
He still loves it
To follow old rules
That made him a man of worth
Crores has he amassed
Wisely placed hither and thither

He would get into the middle
Of his workers and toil
Like one of them
It didn't matter if his attire was soiled
And if he smelt sweat
Which the chiffon called a stink

He would then don
At the end of the day
The tie and jacket hung
On the wall and hurry
Brushing his hair on the way
To clients with cart-loads of deliveries
Invoice book, carbon and pen
Ever ready in his long coat pockets

The pig sat ruminating
Yawned to the grinding tune
Of the grandpa ceiling fan
As the sweating summer afternoon
Sank its way to horizon

The brats are yet to return
And cause commotion
Pandemonium would soon devour
The peace of the house after school hours

Agnes, the maid, moved in like a breeze
Holding his steaming cup of tea
She is their maid ever since
He married the chiffon pack
Brought her home long back

Childless, widowed, she was it
If gentleness had another name
Hailing from Goa she brought in
Peace of beaches, moonlit nights

She did bear the chiffon's whims
Saintly with a distant smile
She could stand the kids' antics
Sagely composed like a stoic

Wherever did she turn her eyes
She saw only Jesus Christ
Her one and only single child
Though she mothered everything

Elsewhere, in an overcrowded hall
Extempore prolific chiffon spat
To unending thunderous applause
Swooning over a big-wig guest
Acclaimed champion of the weaker sex

A perennial wife-beater in secret
He sat stroking his moustache
Ogling the fluttering damsels
And rehearsed the rhetoric stuff
His junior has penned for his address

The lofty stuff the guy fabricates
Has always been beyond his wits
Knowledge he guessed
Never courted success
The junior was evidence
Unknown he remains accursed

As slumber weighed his eyelids down
The pig wished he had married the maid
Guilt soon brought his deity in
To duster the thought off his mind
As he snored his way down in
To the land of peace with no things seen

———

MCP = Male chauvinist pig*

35. He

What use is it to him who is audition to know the ear?
What use is it to him who is sight to know the eye?
What use is it to tactility to concern with the itchy skin?
Of what avail to relish the working of the tongue?

He, who is olfaction, will he yearn for a nose
To smell the fragrance of the blossoming rose?
What use is it to light to know its constant pace
When it pervades everything and every place
In a manner eternal, ineffable, sans time-space?

Salutations to Him!

36. My Response to a 'Programmer's Poem'

(*The poem titled "Programmer's Poem" quoted below is by an unknown author. It was e-mailed to me by my brother during the time the world was going through a financial melt-down a few years ago. My response to it appears below it.*)

Programmer's Poem
(Unknown author)

I start my day by sitting on a chair,
Giving my monitor a hard, cold stare,
By evening I'm done with another coding.
Oh! This has become a routine so boring.

Like all, I entered this field with great hope,
Jobs were many and there was plenty of scope,
Dreams of joining the likes of Gates,
And a chance to make money in the States.

This, I entered the world of bytes,
Only to realize that reality bites.
'Coz a programmer's life, isn't all that cozy.
The bed of software isn't all that rosy.

Seeing the monitor all day n night,
Have taken the power off my eyesight,
Late to bed n late to rise,
Has made me wealthy, but not healthy n wise.

Working holidays, busy weekends.
No time for family, no time for friends,
My job steals most of my time,
Helplessly, I watch this crime.

Just for few bits of money,
I forego those moments with my Honey,
When I should be out - having fun,
I'm telling a comp, what's to be done.

I hate you, yet I can't get away,
'Coz, I need the money u pay.
God, to thee I pray,
If there be one - show me the way.

———————

My Response:

The way has come now in the form
Of global crisis, the killer storm
Shaken to the bottom, out of form
My boss called me just to inform

That he didn't need me any more
And that I am free like before
To roam the streets and go where I wish
Like a forsaken dog and perish

Oh Lord, Oh Lord, I didn't see
When I cursed the monitor Thee
In the glitter all over its face
Were You always smiling at me

Lord of Lords, please give me my job
PC, monitor, my fatigued yawn
Take anything in exchange you want
Wife, kids, home or all that I flaunt!

For I know that I only loved
One and only one so fond
And that is me, the rest don't count
Keep me to the PC always bound

37. HSE, HSE, HSE! *

Hovering over a flashing sign
*At the portal to Ahmadi***
Chirped the fluttering sparrow
To the tiny desert flower
That had just offered
Its first golden smile
To the rising sun of spring:

"Eh, ye! What are these guys upto
Erecting these boards all around
That change colours and scenes
Like lights on a festival ground? "

The flower smiled again,
This time philosophically:
"My flying friend of the sky,
Haven't you yet heard
HSE, HSE, HSE!

"Having all these years,
Burnt and smoked earth and air,
Men choked of breath,
Have now seen some sense
And know for sure
The dance of death awaits
If they don't change their traits."

"Nature, the teacher,
Has taught them the lesson
That they should have known
From day one – but Alas!
They had chosen
The peril of undoing
Their own God-given home."

"Isn't it strange that it took
A hole in the polar skies,
Countless clogged windpipes,
Scarred lungs and hearts,
Scary seas of slick and waste,
Smoky dark afternoons,
Gasping towns asthmatic
For them to understand
The simple truth that the gift of God,
This 'blue marble' of the cosmos
Is a treasure to be preserved,
Be whatever the cost?"

"Listen friend, they have now begun,
Singing a chorus in unison,
"HSE, HSE, HSE!"
In utter repentance and in hope,
Determined to salvage
The oases senselessly ravaged".

"Young men and women
Who put up these signs
Have a vision of what their home
Should be like, unlike the ones
Who rushed before them
Defiling nature's sacred realms
In wanton, hasty sacrilege."

"HSE, HSE, HSE!"
Echoed the sparrow,
As it soared in the brilliant sun,
Buoyed by the February wind,
Hope infused by the flower,
On to a eucalyptus branch
That smelt health and well-being.

A bemused alley cat
That sat under the tree
Wondered what all this joy could be.
Her whiskers rayed out
Untold happiness
Deep from a sunny heart
As she mewed with the wind
"HSE, HSE, HSE!".

"HSE, HSE! " sang the kids
Their voice filled with mirth.
"HSE, HSE" sang the winds
As they hissed and kissed the trees.
"HSE, HSE" sang the heart
As it lay on God's own lap,
Dreaming a world clean and green
Where all His children lived and preened
Letting every creature live
In peace, endowed with healthy breath,
Safe and secure without care
"HSE, HSE, HSE! "

––––––––––

*HSE = Health, Safety and Environment
* * Ahmadi is an oil town in Kuwait

38. Lamp-Boy

A tree silhouetted against
The silver winter sky
And setting crimson Sun
On the canvas of consciousness
An exalting sight

The impatient artist
Then moved the screen
Lo, the black night dawned
Speckled with a million dots

He then packed his palette
Left the place
Leaving me the lamp-boy
In my aloneness
To light the canvas
Throughout the night

39. Newspaper and a Broken Back

There was a time
Picking the newspaper from the door-steps
Was great pleasure
The headlines were thrillers

Alas, today
An ad of a cell-phone full-page
A new car or a television stares
From all over the front page
And the headlines
Mostly in insipid language
Are buried deep inside

And as you carry the paper
Inside to pick your lenses
There is a diarrhoea of flyers
Loosely inserted
Which scatter here and there
In the wind of the fan
Together with the city supplement
Of pure nonsense
On celebrities and film stars
In no time you are
A squatting scavenger

Own your dream homes
They are everywhere
At easy prices
Or just go on holiday
Flight and hotel included
Incredibly discounted

Why not buy a microwave
That has functions you know not
Meant for some unknown recipe
Of the Caribbean
Or is it Polynesian?

Own a fridge rather
Never loses its cool
That is low on power
Innumerable advantages
Storage ingeniously designed

Send your kids to Yoga classes
Supervised by American teachers
Cleanse their bodies and souls
Spiritual prowess at doorstep

Lo, the India of ours
Is a real paradise
Of dream houses and holidays
Teachers, doctors, match-makers
There is everything available
Just for tuppence
Why not sit back, close your eyes
Utopia is your birth-right

And I did sit back
With the paper in hand
On the grand new sofa
Put together somewhere in Indonesia
Which we bought the other day
At a very discounted price
Made my wife's esteem rise
In her spiralling friend circles

I didn't have time to reach
The headlines 'ere which the legs gave in
Poor thing couldn't stand the Indian weight!
The rest of the story
My ortho will narrate
I am living in his paradise
Of course for a cheap price

He too had a flyer inserted
In the same rag I was about to read
Which I am yet to see
But for my broken spine

40. Blackie, Blackie, Where Are You?

The Lady of the house, bespectacled
Shades her eyes, calls out
Blackie, Blackie, where are you?
A call as sure as an alarm pre-set

She just finished a party
A grand dinner and the invitees
Have trickled out one by one
Leaving the house all alone

Her calls rouse me from slumber
At the base of the chimney
In its shadow cast by the waxing moon
Time I got up and hurried
To feast on the sumptuous left-over
She has set aside for me
To which no other cats are privy

She is the only one
Who has time for me
Party or no party
Work or holiday
Her calls would resonate
Three times a day
Blackie, Blackie, where are you?

And I from my slumber would move
Meowing my way
Down the sloping wall
To the back of the house
Where she would be waiting impatient
Her hands on her hips
To see me feast through her thick lenses

Why is she so fond of me?
Why is it that she has such softness
For this stray Blackie alone
When there are house-cats
Beautiful like dolls
To be bought from the market-place?

God alone has the answer
Or why worry about such questions
Profound and existential?
It is granted she likes Blackie
Why split my hair or her genes
Seeking an answer
Or why proposition a carry forward
From impervious previous lives?

She is so different
I love her and her bespectacled look
A real madam who the moustached brute
Of the house, overweight
With a mighty paunch
Doesn't deserve
Even in a hundred lives

He detests cats
Calls me stray
Shoos me away
Out of sight always

And the boy of the house
Again thickly bespectacled
Pouring over books
Day and night
Has no time for cats
Or even his food
What is it that he mugs
Up so late into the night?
Does what he reads tell
More about life
Than a stray cat sees
With its open eyes?

And, lo, the beautiful girl
She always has a phone
Over her ears, lost to the world
Has no eyes even to the things
That lie next to her
Why do they live
So closed to the world
Clammed up in their private shells?

No answer why I alone
Ponder such questions
Into the depths of nights
Looking at the moon
Languishing in the phantom shade
Of an unthinking nosy chimney

When down on the roads
Death is on the prowl
In the form of speeding cars
Wheeled by care-free dare-devils
Which have crushed
My innocent babes and a lot of my ilk

Who does understand
The insecurity of a cat
Stray as it is
On vagrant streets?

Perhaps, the lady down does
And her calls reverberate
Inside me or is it me
Calling out to me
From deep within me
Blackie, Blackie, where are you?
An answerless existential poser

41. Jasmine Bud

She came last night
Lay right on this bed
The wind outside my window
Paused its impatient rustle

She slept and dreamed
Soft and cool
Her eyes were dew drops
Closed and guarded
By dense black lashes

Who could venture
What she saw
Inside there
In that prismatic vibgyor
Unearthly images that could be
An envy even for angels heavenly

She slept like a figurine
Chiseled out of the mist
The curls of her tresses
The moon cautiously fondled
Pouring herself like liquid
Through undulating curtain slits

I sat by her side
On nightlong vigil
Moving not lest she awakes
In total adoration
Absorbed in delight
Till I heard the chirps

By when she had been gone
Dissolved like morning mist
Vanished in thin air
Was that a dream?
I can't figure

Yet, there is this jasmine bud
Left on the bed
Proof for a dream that was real
That had just passed
Pouring sadness in the heart
Oh, what is real and unreal?

I dare not touch the bud
Lest it too vanishes
From my flimsy hold
Wonted all the time to losses alone

42. I Saw Them Walking

I saw them walking
Along the forlorn street
At night against my headlights
Hand in hand together
Whispering into each other

The east wind had just begun
To whisper to the leaves
In hush hush
And what could be these love-birds
Crooning into the ears of each other?

What could the chill of the night
Hold for them - a distant hut
Where dreams are made
With the feathers of paradise?

Take a bit of me at least
Into your thoughts
When you share your warmth tonight
Love birds in your nest
So that my night is made
Sweet with the east wind
And soulful solitude
Aloneness sans any bounds

43. Please Let Him Hurl

A boy
Hardly five
Threw a tomato at me
On a crowded Tamil street
It hit my chest and splashed
A constellation of yellow stars
On my blue T-shirt

His mother admonished
And chided him in harsh words
She poured herself on me
With profuse apology

I told her not to worry
Her ward didn't do anything wrong
He might bowl for the country
In the future and bring laurels
In international cricket

Or rather he will pick cudgels
And hit out against injustice
When a mother or sister
Or the weak or underprivileged
Is violated on our uncertain land

Keep him hurling mom
And let him grow
So that our weaknesses
And unjust excesses
Never go unopposed
Or unanswered

Let the spark in him
Be a brilliant flame
And guide us ahead
With its splashy glow

44. Happy Birthday!

Yesterday I turned sixty-one
And someone long forgotten
Sent me a mail wishing hundred and one
An expression of habitual sentiment

*He knew I loved our Mother**
For he cared to attach Her snap.
Her lips were a bewitching smile
Folded hands were soulful prayer
For us all who have no time for Her

Viewed the picture, a glance sufficed
Oh, my disk has no more space
The mail found its way to trash
Who has time for wishing farce?

Another day of dreary chores
Frenzied phone calls, business talks
Ceaseless standing on the toes
Back to PC at the close

The old always guides
I look for a document saved
For help in having a new one made
Don't we always retrieve the buried! ?

Lo! What could be this, a new file
In 'My Documents' saved
Without my knowledge?
Finger curiously clicks

The smile brightens the screen
Like the dawn of spring-time sheen
Hands fold again to greet
A careless son so indiscrete

For all I know I had pressed "Delete"
Nevertheless She refused to retreat
At the bottom of our being, isn't it
"My Documents" - Her sacred retreat?

A tear-drop tiny grows and wells
In my erstwhile blinded eyes
To spark an insight so very bright
"A Mother never ever leaves Her kids"

———————

** a saintly lady*

45. Basic Units of Science

When I said I weighed seventy kilos
I didn't bother I weighed seventy times
The weight of an alloy cylinder
Made of platinum and iridium
Preserved near Paris at Sevres

To it the physicist so far clung
When he measured the weight of things
Like a life-boat on choppy seas
And alas today he is dismayed
The thing at Sevres can no more be guide
Everything is subject to change
Environment and wear and tear
Presided over by tyrant time
The cylinder sure has lost some weight
Despite careful handling strict

The need of the hour, nay minute
Is therefore to redefine weight
How can that be ever done
If we are to design matter alone
When change through time afflicts
Everything at every place?

An insurmountable conundrum indeed
Over-awed brains are losing sleep
"We have no problem" someone quipped
'With distance, say a meter, as it is
Measured against the speed of light
A natural constant without change
Unlike the sanctified alloy piece"

He didn't bother the pace of light
Is reckoned against plaguing time
Whose unit the second derives
Sustenance from matter atomic
Of a particular type
In a particular state
In transition betwixt
Two levels hyperfine

Back to square one that is
A vicious circle indeed!
How could one ever rely
On matter alone to define
The basic units of science?

Caught we are in a flux
Trying to make sense
Lost like a ship in mid-seas
With no land or star in sight

Yet so sure are we

That we are right

To think that light escapes

The tyranny of time and change

Unaware of the Light that shines

Light and the constructs of space and time

46. Special Eyesight

God granted me last night
Special super-fine eyesight
That excelled the range
Of the best electron microscope

I was thrilled and looked around
Nothing at all solid was found
No familiar names and forms
Not anything known as things
Particles flew in empty space
Pervaded by a Rontgen glow

I still felt I had a body
But it was of no avail
My face with an ugly scar
That had eaten deep and deep
Into my sinking self-esteem
And made me suffer misery
Was no more there for me to see

The buxom beauties
That walked the ramps
At the world beauty pageant
Were just conglomerates
Indistinct from one another
Of flashing points
And no different
From the beggar women
In utter tatters
That walk our city streets

No one had any reason
To feel any different
And removed from one another
No more wars
The borders have gone
No more sickness
The organs too have gone

Everything was nothing but
Flashing particles flying
In a fluorescent mist of light
No sun no moon not a star
No ground at all to stand upon

Hung helpless in that void
I cried out to the supreme Lord
Please give me my ignorance back
With my familiar vision range
So I see my forms with names

I heard God laugh and thunder
Who said your ignorance is asunder
Just be there and watch the fun
You are going to wrap around
One of the particles flying by

Bound you are and limited still
Different from other dots in flight
Your scar will return and you will sink
Again into abysmal grief
In a new world that is filled
With names and forms of your own make
Unless of course you can cease
Your usual blabber of I and mine

47. Blessed Be Your Sons

I walked down a Tamil street
Drunken of the elements
Cold gushing gales inebriate
As it poured cats and dogs
On the west beyond the Ghats

Winds and clouds embraced
Each other in passion
In the rain-shadow where I trod
It drizzled as the sky bristled
Unshaven above looming dark
Pretentious of a downpour

Jutting onto the street
On my meandering path
A Devi temple stood
Painted gaudy green and red
Where the destitute waited
Extending their shrivelled palms
For sporadic drop of alms

And there sat this old woman
A bag of bones
Mass of wrinkles with grey hair
Like a puffy summer cloud
Cotton candy on a stick
Hung in the present without a past
Untouched by time gazing past

I sat beside her
Called her my mother
For she couldn't be anything else
For a man out on the streets
Drunken with soulful forlornness
Sweetened by monsoon rains and winds

I fed her my morsels
Gave her the coins
She smiled in wrinkles
Just enough for a son
As I walked back
In drunken ataxia
Soaked in tears
To my temporary shelter
Of worldly impatience
And frowning grimace

The nest of the heart
Now has a hatching egg
Of hopeful awareness
That the Mother is around
Every which way one turned
To remind us of Her presence
Come home Mother in countless numbers
And bless us your wandering sons

48. Columbia Blossoms

(Written when space shuttle Columbia crashed with Kalpana Chawla on board)

They streaked blazing a trail
Across Awareness that is Thee
Seven petals on to Your Lotus Feet!

Eyes welling, Ma, here I place
Shining rain drops on Your Feet!
For we are the cloudless sky
So blessed to rain
Roses and tears alike

Keep us raining in peace
Unabated at Your wish
Sons and daughters as You please!

Peace, Peace, Peace!

49. Nang Nak

Last night I watched the movie "Nang Nak"
The hero returns home after a war
Lives with the ghosts of his wife and baby
Unaware they had died while he fought far away

And then when I turned around
I saw only ghosts abound
Non-real beings, planets, stars
All that my universe bore
And at last, my body and thoughts
Dancing apparitions in swirls
Frenzied dervishes in whirls

I prayed at the feet of the Buddha
Bewildered by spectral samsaara
Did He smile at last?
Or a non-real thought that was?

Or does it matter at all?
That I know is proof after all
That I exist to validate
Real, unreal, non-real
Like a glow that reveals
Self-iridescence concealed

And here I lie now erased
Of body, mind and the seen
A void that has everything
Sans forms and names
And yet the fullest thing
A Buddha living in everything

50. A Flight Out of the Taittiriya* Mesh

Oh Lord! How much I wish
I hadn't said anything
*On this wordy Taittiriya mesh**
That entraps our thoughts
And clips their wings!

It all began
With an innocent query
On the lofty Upanishad
See, where it has taken
With heated debates
Well-armed players on stage
The asker having gone
Leaving not a trace

There was this man
Who asked 'What is the Truth? '
Placed amidst the manifest
Rootlessly perplexed
The means of knowledge he held
Could only tell
What is what
And how things apparently worked

Working day and night
Sparing not a minute
Pouring over the microscope
Straining on the telescope
Reached he nowhere
And wondered aloud
What could possibly be
The end of this unending game

His means held him good
Many a law and rule he made
Theories and theorems split his hair
Made him gasp for air
Yet, every night he retired
The unanswered poser remained
Lord, what all this I see could be?

The wise told him:
"Eh ye, behold!
This is all One
And that is the Truth
You are caught
In a whirlpool
Of the manifest
Your pitiful domain
Of toil and sweat
Labour, love and lust! "

"What you need is a boat
That can cut across
The whirl's cruel centrifugal hold
And take you ashore
To yonder glittering Land
Where the Sun of Truth shines
In His timeless magnificence"

"Where is the boat, Oh, Sages? "
Asked the lost
"I see only the diverse
Split in so many ways
Well numbered, tagged and named
In an infinite endless surge
Which I can't hope to bound"

"Read and listen" said the wise
"Search with your inner eyes"
Threw they tomes at him
A sea of words sublime
"Hearken, ye! The blind!
Here is the scripture for you
Means for the End
Domain eternal, the peaceful Land"

Days without number he poured
Over the million sacred words
Into the quest he put
Soul, heart and endless thirst
At last, when he raised his head
The smiling sages heard him ask:

"Oh, wise men, I haven't seen
Any glittering land or domain
I had before a set of rules
Well defined for the work I do
You have added more to it
And made my quest chaotic"

"If there is a domain other than mine
Does it mean that we have twain?
Words of wisdom, tomes you rained
Aren't they very much in this mine
This very manifest you want me leave? "

"Tell me, masters, how they are
Means for yet another domain
Who in his sense would ask for one
When he and the scripture are in this one
Face to face, in tight embrace? "

The sages left him overawed
Scratching their beards guffawed:
"Who could imagine there could be
Impervious souls so much over-flawed!
Leave him in his hell and let us
Make for snow-clad peaks of peace! "

The Ganges swirls of the manifest
Roared around in frenetic haste
Lost in a brood, the man realized
Inseparable in her caressing grip
Were he and the scripture, her own babes

The whirls danced unabated
Till at last a surging love
From nowhere whispered:
In his pining ears: "Son dear,
Can you ever be
Other than me, the manifest? "

He was the dance, he was the swirl,

He was the world's torrential flow

That needed not know land or shore

Suns or domains afar any more

He was the scripture free of worry

Light of the manifest with all means buried!

** Taittiriya Upanishad - an ancient Indian philosophical text that probes into the substantive of the manifest universe*

51. Orphanage

Across the river
Along my way
Between home and school
There was an orphanage

Children used to frolic
There in sheer abandon
Oblivious
Of their parentless misfortune

Some among them were blind
Others deaf
Some handicapped
Yet they were happy
As though on a merry-go-round
Filled to the brim with joy

The warden then had said
With moist eyes
Look boy, this is a temple
Bapu once sat
Right under that mango tree
Looking at the children play
With a toothless smile
This is no orphanage
The kids have the nation's parentage

More than fifty years thence
I crossed the same river
Now totally desecrated
In every sense
It no more had
The sugary sand beds
Of the past
To boast about

She lay weeping
In rationed tears
Bunded at every place
By greedy farmers
Abandoned by the rains
Sacrileged by stinking drains

The orphanage had gone
And there was a bar
Of four or five stars
With glittering lights
Right at its place

I asked a passerby
What happened
To the nest of the past
That sheltered
The wingless birds

Orphanage?
He sneered
Well, look, that place
Belongs to our leader
A socialist to the hilt
A philanthropist right to core
Whose father
Was a freedom fighter

Yonder across the street
He built that magnificent temple
For Mother Durga
Where we prostrate
Morning and evening
Blessed is he
Would have built the shrine
Right here close to the bar
Hadn't stupid laws of the land
Wanted a distance
Between prayer and bar

He is great
Of secular mind
Employs several hands
Of every faith
The CM of the State
Dines at his house
When in town
Don't waste your time
Over the ones
That vanished
With an orphanage

I looked around in vain
No care center was found
On the ancient land of mine
That instilled in the mind
A sense of national parentage

If there were any
By the name
They were labeled
By faith and creed
Where no Indians frolicked
No mango-tree to sight
With a Bapu under it

And as I looked around
I saw only orphans abound
Orphaned of parentage
Orphaned of virtues
Orphaned of values
And orphaned at last of God
By whom all of them swore

Orphaned of love for their land
Orphaned of their motherland
Though they all swore
By Durga divine
Loudly by the Virgin
Or by some other saint
Utterly fossilized
In sectarian concrete

Oh, how much I wish
Bapu was there
And sat in the shade
Of a spreading tree
Smiling his toothless smile
At this teeming orphanage
That shames a nation's name

Then comes a passerby
Who says he saw
The statue of Bapu weep
At the city square
In the wee hours

An orphan rejoined
No, that was no tears
But the setting moon
Shining on morning dew
Upon granite stone

He was a rationalist
Votary of progress
That is make-believe
Who swore by science
And reasoning
But forsook his heart
To languish in
A self-made orphanage
And missed the spirit
That made nations click

52. Dream Dance

They were two thugs
Tough men
Who fought for their territory
Like animals in jungles

One had settled there before
The other one came later
Both ferocious like tigers
Muscles had the deciding power

They came out of their abodes
Showered abuses on each other
Insecure the other guy might win
Reason to be cautious

Their words were acid, vituperative
Yet, they dared not take
The duel to a physical level
Aren't all our heroes
After all silly cowards?

Then they found a rhythm
In their vociferous exchange
Something their dithering feet
Could emulate
There was an element of dance
And measure
Even in mutual mud-slinging

And they danced
The two thugs
Engaged in a wordy duel
Vituperative like volcanoes
Throwing lava on each other

The villagers saw them dance
Joined in, women and kids
In sheer abandon
The whole place danced

What a splendorous beauty that was
That began in a duel
Of enmity and ended
In absolute felicity
Of great abandon of the feet

The thugs danced
As did the villagers
And then the whole world
Joined in, black and white
Brown who took themselves white
Oh, that was a sea of mirth
Frothing, brimming out of bounds

And then came the tidal wave
Of animals of all sorts
From nearby jungles
They all danced
Like never before
In rare camaraderie

Lo, the deer and wildcats together
Antelopes, lions and tigers
And the trumpeting pachyderms
No one knows what got into their heads
They moved in a swirl
That shamed dervishes everywhere
Oh, could this be our world! ?

And then I awoke
That was a dream
That came from far of heavens
Early in the morning at five O'clock

I rolled on my bed restless
I had all the dance
Still in my waking senses
Yet, I can't make it happen again
For, I am condemned to be human
In a world where friends can't be
Only at each other's throat could we be

53. Man's Best Friend

Rain clouds ran berserk on the hills
Like elephant herds in panic
Winds whistled like villains
On the winding mountain pass

A warm tea would do me good
I stopped my car and moved
Towards a dilapidated shed
Where men of all shades
Huddled together puffing beedies

He came after me then
His eyes had a moist glisten
Of ageless friendship
Wagging his tail looking up
At me, placing his paws on my thighs

Stray dog of the mountain pass
His eyes were mascara lined
A beauty to behold
A silky brownness filled with mirth
And wavy musculature

What does he like?
Anything, Sir, that we have here
I bought him a sweet bun
He gulped it at once
Wagging his tail again
Ageless camaraderie in his eyes

I bought him a second bun
Before I drained
The last drops of my steaming tea
Made from what God knows
On that forsaken mountain pass

And as I walked back to my car
In an elemental swirl
Of winds, drizzle, mist and clouds
He was there behind me
With that haunting friendship in his eyes

Friend, our knowing each other
Is perhaps endless
It never had a beginning either
We were together through ages
Births, rebirths, deaths and pangs

Perhaps, you guarded my Neanderthal cave
When I snored inside
Looking at the Moon and wondering
Why the world was made
So beautiful to behold

Or perhaps you sat there in the snow
Outside my igloo freezing
Looked at the white expanse and mused
Why it had to be so awesome
When it bit into the bones
And stiffened the looks even
Of the stars in the heavens

Adieu friend, we are to meet
Again and again in our sojourns
Keep the friendship burning
In your moist eyes, sure am I
You will be there when I breathe
My last on some mountain pass
Sitting at my head, man's best friend
What more would a human want?

54. Che

In my hometown
At a busy intersection
They have placed
A bust of yours, Che

Kids ask who this is
Their parents know not who he is
They mumble nonsense
The kids look perplexed

Then there are the young ones
Who speed on bikes
High on Indian hash
Overrun unfortunate puppies
And kitten on the road
During evening rush hour
Which they think
Is a revolution of sort

They have your image
On their T-Shirts
They know not who you are
But just Che – a nobody
From wilderness
Who stirred emotions
Somewhere in Bolivia
And in Latin America
Where kitchens didn't burn
But only stomachs

On this rainy day
When skeletal remains
Of starving humanity
Wail across the globe
Like overrun kitten and puppies
Che, lemme prostrate
Before your bust
And call you, dear friend of Nerudu

Please keep coming back
To blast the bastions
Of the Batistas
We need your fire
Intelligence and power
To deliver us from the yoke
However unending the task

They might sever your hands
Parcel them to lands
To terrorize those
Who straighten their spines
But do please keep coming back
Che, so that our kids know
Who Guevara was
And don his mantle

Che, please keep igniting the fire
Of an oppressed fraternity
This lonely cold rainy night
Of looming darkness and pain
So men rise again
To confront guns and pain
With unbending steel-like spine

55. A Prayer to Ramana

Oh, brilliant eyes!
Yet to blossom smile!
Visage profoundly serene!
Show me the way sublime

Out of this mesh much knotted
In which I am woefully trapped
Made of mind and intellect
Understanding and what not

Of teachers by whom I aver
Of books I don't close ever
Of a body demanding care
Of senses gone haywire

I know all these to be
Not me, because them I do see
Yet, I know not the seeing me
For blind is my inner eye

"All you know is you are not,
What knows is you" I am taught
'Knowing this much will suffice
You then are self-realized'

"A mere understanding, isn't this? "
I question losing all my wits
"Yes, it is so by all the means
It does take place in the mind"

"Isn't mind in knowing? " I ask
"So what? " "The wise does think" they remark
"The wise does act, the wise does read
The wise does enjoy the food he eats"

"Granted all that" I concede
"The wise knows not that he reads
That he acts and that he eats
The way we do so incomplete"

Didn't our Sage say the wise is like
One in himself fast asleep
On a shaky cart on potholed track
Knowing not the shocking creaks

My soulful plea therefore Lord Ramana
Dear Sage of Holy Arunachala!
Cast your kind glance upon me
Truth of "Who am I? " so I see

So I realize what it is like
Being in this tumultuous sea
Knowing and yet knowing not
Knowing all as me in me

Soaring up and up the sky
Wingless, mindless, ever-free
Unbridled by whims of intellect
Unburdened by notions pet

In the sky of Pure Being
To which Your eyes beckon,
To the beauty of spaceless expanse
Where Your smile shines and awakens

56. Vancouver

Where am I to find your soul
Oh, Vancouver, where are you?

In your magnificent parks
Downtown symmetry of beautiful roads
Speeding sky-trains sliding smooth
North, south east and west
On sky-rise mansions that shine back the sun?

Where are you?

I missed you wherever I looked
Like the elusive maple
Hard to spot in your famous parks
Just dry leaves here and there
Then on paper
Proud image of State power.

Vancouver, where are you?

The grey of the sky, rain-soaked wet
Bite of chilly winds from west
Had no answer to offer
Neither did cherry-blossoms
That rain splendour on the roads
And passers-by
So profusely

Vancouver, where am I to find your soul?

I looked for you in the shine
Of lovers' eyes in embrace, in vain,
In walkers who throw gentle smiles
On passers-by, yet aloof by miles
In the childlike demeanour of the aged
Meandering your parks their past packaged

I asked the firs, acacia, pines
Cypress, magnolia, evergreens
Giant dogwoods fast asleep
Thoughtful spruces, cedars alike
They offered a pre-spring yawn
Clad still smug in winter yarns

Silent, cold was Seymour Creek
Mist on Fraser did not speak
Ice-capped peaks on north and south
Neither had a word to mouth
Nothing on the landscape revealed
Where Vancouver remained concealed

Where am I to find your soul?
Oh, Vancouver, where are you?

At last as I emplane home,
I am beckoned from the groves
By you, Vancouver, there you are
In the sprouts that dot the barks -
Budding foliage - spring embarks!

You are the one soul that sustains
Winter's silence, mirth of spring
Like sleep and wake in single chain
In me, Oh, we never are twain
Sad I missed you so many times!

57. Wheelchair Might

Get on the wheelchair
Bypass the immigration mire
Have your way swift
Through security check
Pretend you are disabled
Be an object of pity
Drag your feet
Like beggars on Bombay streets

Or put your parents on wheelchair
Even if they are like athletes fit
Gobble tonnes of sweets
Without the blood sugar
Rising even a wee bit

Then escort them in and out
Laughing at the toilers behind
Who wait in long lines
At indifferent counters
Wiping sweating foreheads
Cursing unmoving watches
Idiots who don't realize
Craftiness they should devise
If quick success is the end in sight

This my friend is the secret
To success in the world
Do not ever be sentimental
Follow this everywhere
Thou shan't grieve
Born thou art to survive

Put your candidates on wheelchair
Contest elections to parliament
Why not even have the chair
As election symbol
You will win for sure
Riding the sympathy wave
A tear-box is any time proof
Even against popular tides

And as you wheel your easy way out
Of the world's numberless airports
Your head clogged with the dream
Of owning a wheelchair business in boom
Don't forget to wink without shame
At those who still stay behind
Whose rights you have infringed

The gracefully aging ones
Octogenarians and nonagenarians
Alike of the world's every nook and corner
Still waiting at the belts
For their baggage to arrive
Their spines held steady like steel
Shaming all the metal you wheel
Who still find ardour
In their fast aging vigour

58. Ode to Tsunami

You came uncalled
To sweep us in your folds
And drag us to depths unknown
You came uncalled
To crush our dreams
And snatch treasures
From our helpless hold

Tsunami! We had heard of you
In our school days
As one striking far off lands
And seen you in movies
That our wizards make
To fill their coffers full
As a speeding wall
That makes humans flee
To the safety of mountain heights

But never even in the worst
Of our nightmares
Did we ever suspect
You would give us a breakfast call
To smash our little tea-cups
Filled with care and mirth
And topple sunshades of comfort
Along havens we frequent
To watch delightful sunsets

Never did we suspect
You are ruthless and careless
To wipe off the ones
Who look at the sun
And plead every morn
For nothing but light alone

Tsunami, why were you
So unkind and cruel
Even to babes
Hugging their moms
In blissful slumber
In forlorn huts
Along our golden coasts?

You are madness unleashed
To upend our dreams
Upturned on a brittle world
Where no more are granted
Method, trust and certitude

For we now suspect the breeze
For the storm, the murmur of the sea
For dangers unknown
Whose bosom with carefree ease
Our folks used to fathom
For pearls and wisdom
From days unknown.

The sea was our mother
And now she has frowned
The wrinkles on her face
Make us shudder and flee
Like ants before the storm
On to safer yet uncertain planes

A delight on our TV screens,
Tsunami, overnight
You have become a mortal fright
We dare no more entertain
Faith on this lonely oasis
Of the cosmos, where till you came
Certainty was our walking stick

Roofless in these wintry nights
While we shiver on shaky heights
Of temporary comfort
Away from the seas
A tsunami surges in our hearts
To sing and roar an ancient song

A song of wisdom we forgot
In our haste for false comforts
Rampage for wealth and might
Powered by false sense of right
Blood for blood we paid
Head for head we reaped
And shamed the beasts we caged

For we were cocksure
All morns are full of sunshine
Just made for our comfort
For we took it granted
Paradise was our right
Till you came, Tsunami
With your teaching stick

We call you an act of God
And yet pursue our erstwhile wont
As though it is all that He wants
We count the pennies lost
As we rummage our flattened coasts
And rebuild the resorts lost
Shedding tears for have-nots
Lo, bereft our inside lies
Lost of the Light that shines
Tsunamis and the like
Alike like sunshine and delight

Teach us, tsunami, again
Waving your powerful whip
That shine and cloud are alike
So are feared death and birth
In the bosom of the Lord
Where breeze and hurricane originate

Sing your song again and again
To our mortal deafness
So we hearken
To the Godness we are
So we don't shiver
And mourn when again
Our morns fail to shine

Make us sing this song
Again and again
So we shall face
With a tight upper-lip
The destiny of the dinosaurs
If He so wills
For, we then no more fear
Extinction on this oasis
As we sure will survive
As the spark that shines
The world and the tsunami you

59. A Drunkard's Song

When am I not drunk
Jesus Christ?
When am I not drunk of the love for You
Jesus Christ?

When am I not pained?
When am I not drunk of the pain You bore
On the Cross, Jesus Christ?

When am I not loved?
When am I not blessed?
When am I not drunk
Of the love that You showered on earth
Jesus Christ?

Am not a Christian
Born to Christian parents
But Christ, mind You my mentor
Since You can't be sectarian
For love has no religious taint
I am just a drunkard
Drunk of universal love
Wasn't that the pain You bore
For all of us
On the Cross?

Sink down therefore into my veins
As they mount me on a Cross
Calling me a drunkard
A drunkard of love
Oh, Jesus Christ!

I would be there in the fiery sun
On a dusty desert plain
Filled with bliss
Please mount me on the Cross
Hammer nails into me
I would look at the horizon
The salty sweat on my eyebrows
Would still look for you
My mentor, the salvation
I am a drunkard
Drunk of love
Jesus Christ!

60. King Elephant

The elephant of our village temple
Passed away the other day
We drowned in sorrow
It was a dark day
Every eye was deluged
Every heart painfully bled

He was a pet of all
Kids loved him most
Stood holding his trunk
Posing for photographs
He had all the auspicious marks
To make him a cynosure of eyes

Other animals like dogs and cows
Took him in confidence
Moved close to him
Without fear
He spoke love
Spontaneous natural
He was a marvel
Though he was animal

He always held
The central position
In festive processions
His head always held high
Like a peak in a mountain range

The idols of deities
Always liked
His mammoth gait
Animal might and height
As he strode
Carrying them on his back
Bell below his neck ringing
Hilly temple raised
Against the brilliant sky
During their auspicious go-arounds
Every morning and evening

He was named
The King Of Kings
Rightly so he was a king
Of unsurpassed excellence, supreme
The land wept his death
For it loved him so much
From the bottom of the heart

Posters came up at every corner
Of the town and around
Paying tributes
To his divine attributes
There was spontaneous grief
All eyes bore testimony
As they welled
In profuse wetness
Like overflowing ponds
In monsoon rains

How is it that an animal's death
Goes so touchingly lachrymose
In so much pain and longing?
What is it in the Indian psyche
That strikes such tearful empathy
With nature and her siblings?

When everything sacred
Brother, sister, mother and father
Are raped and trespassed
Humiliated, tortured
Trampled in wanton disregard
Of basic human values?

When everything living
That can't speak
Is slaughtered every second
To satisfy
The gluttonous craving
Of insatiable palates?

Isn't there a mammoth
Of goodness lying
In our psyche -
A giant that waits
For our call to be aroused
Dormant like a mountain
Slumbering in darkness?

Oh, sleeping tusker
Gigantic soul of godliness!
Leave your sleep and rise
Make us cry
Again and again
To wash our sins
We, the Indians
Are awaiting here
Steeped in chaotic decadence
The arrival of a savior
To lead us ahead

We will caparison you in gold
March with you
In colorful procession
With drum-beats, fireworks
Pipe-music playing celestial tunes
To the shrine of our beloved Goddess
The temple of Mother India
Ancient and eternal
As old as our godly Ganges

Awake, open your eyes, King!
Raise your trunk and trumpet
To the world around -
The Indians are coming
The long-lost, long-suppressed
Indians are coming again
To unshackle their Mother
Like they did more than
Six decades before

To usher in a new age
Of universal love and peace
On an ancient land
Where every mother
Sister and brother
Child and the aged
Lives fearless
With head held high
Like your upheld forehead
Of honor and might

61. End of the World

I came into this world
They say
So the world was there
When I came in
Where did I come from
Was it another world
Did it end
When I fled
Why should I break my head

The world ends
Every night when I switch off
Yet I close my eyes
Longing for rest
Without worry
Why should I therefore rue
If this one before my eyes
Perishes now or survives

It is there for my eyes to see
Senses to perceive
All in order without an error
Run by impeccable laws
Without my asking
Or prodding
Yet why is it that I worry
If it ends
Without a warning
When something ought to remain
If my nature is to see and grin

What is this world that I worry
So much about
Is it the stars that shine in the Milky Way
Or the galaxies that speed away
Nay not a way
It is my immediate woman
With her youth intact
Merry relatives
Frolicking in unending sunshine
Of a well-to-do spring
The unaccounted filth stashed away
In clandestine accounts
In distant lands
And all that I hadn't had before
But now boastfully brandish

I came into this world
They say
Empty-handed
Without all this that I think are mine
Yet why is it that I worry and break my head
If all this that has come is to slip away

And if the world perishes
Into a lifeless mass
Who would be there
To say "Oh, ye, behold, these are the ashes
The mortal remains
Of our beloved mother earth
Let us just join and look for a Ganges
To flow them and give her peace
In her eternal abode"

Who would say that
Other than me
The intelligence that pulsates
Ever and ever
For the words "I see"
To sprout
Like a waking shoot out of an immortal seed

So let the volcanoes spew
Fire into the skies
Let auroras blaze
Lightnings streak
Thunder roar
Let polar ice melt and tsunamis rise
To submerge the fiery mounts
And quench their thirst

Let God have a Diwali bash
Lighting daisy wheels
Of colourful splendour
Igniting the stars
HE deserves it
Poor guy bored to the core
Having all these days
Patiently kept
The sun, moon and winds on course
All for this unthinking insecure ass

Oh, let the world come to an end
And let me say to my surprise
"I see the world has come to an end"

62. Body and the Universe

(Inspired by a poem by Turkish Sufi poet, Eunus Emre)

Close your eyes and still,
Feel your body
Part by part

And, as you begin to drown
In slumber's sweet embrace
Mountains pop up
As do vales, waterfalls
Green trees, vast landscapes
Stars and the Milky Way

The body is all that
Part by part!
The body is the Universe
You are the body
And you are all!

A magnificent pulsation
Without parts and
Without a beyond!
Be just aware
And remain
Your own ecstatic Self

63. Free Will

Oh Teacher, you taught me
This phenomenal of mine
Is the result of ignorance
Primal and beginningless

Then you taught
I could, I needn't
And I could differently
Isn't what you taught
Ignorance again
Beloved Sage
For it all is in the phenomenal?

Then, tell me, Sir
Why all these intelligent brains
Gray as well as green
In our midst do overtime
To substantiate or refute
A fallacy born of darkness absolute?

They do so every year
Like pollen fever every spring
No topic ever has attracted
So many colourful writings
So differently distracted

Phenomenal is an appearance
You did thunder
In our yearning ears
Isn't free will seeming, Sir
May I add a rejoinder?
Don't take me a pretender

A world seems to erupt
In all its myriad colours
Before my eyes
As I move as the Lord
Pulls the unseen strings
A puppet show
Where I am nothing
Yet I think I have something!
Ignorance of the sublimest kind!

64. Ode to Sachin

A banner in a remote village of Kerala
Greets the worthy son of Maharashtra
Fluttering in the mountain breeze
His smile excels the morning sunshine

A teenage fan of Sachin
In that tribal hinterland
Had hung the banner aloft
On swaying tree tops
As the hero of her heart
Was all set to begin
His last test innings
In far-off Mumbai miles across

Her love for the star was evident
In the manner the passing winds
Fondled his gleaming visage
No doubt what connected the fan
And Sachin across miles of the land
Was the breeze that flowed unseen
The breath of the Nation
A profound Indianness
Born out of centuries
Of lovely cultural co-existence

Whether he scored a ton

Or a lesser yet precious seventy four

Sachin once again proved

He could bind the Nation

Keep it spell-bound

Together in a fondly clasp

A feat not a single soul

Of our land can these days

Dare claim to perform

Be he a leader or a saint

Faith, age, language

Or region had no place

In this adhesive embrace

Which the magic of Sachin spun

As the Nation listened to his farewell address

With bated breath, thumping heart

And overflowing eyes

They would replay the speech again and again

Be together and shed tears

For days and days to come

So their India will sure endure

Held together by an eternal bond

Sachin, you batted in days
When the game got commercialized
By money-makers who reduced
The number of overs to suit their whims
Flouted discipline and rules
Made pawns out of batsmen
Who hit left and right to spin their tons
Like buffaloes let lose in muddy ponds

You stood the tide
Never pawned your artistry
Immaculate form and grace
Dedication and punctuality
In a manner resolute
Acclaimed internationally
Played the game with the demeanor
Of great Englishmen of yore
Least swayed by the luring machinations
Of the greedy who indulged
In match-fixing deals
And got embroiled in politics and scandals
Involving women, loot and wine

You proved yourself
A great son of India
Akin to the Mahatma
A role-model for the new generation
A beacon that should now
Show the way and lead them ahead
To their destiny in togetherness

The Nation roars in unison
Sachin can't retire and leave
He is the fittest person to lead
Having his mettle doubtlessly proved

★ 197 ★

The mantle of the Nation
Has fallen on your shoulders
The mandate has never been so clear
So pick the new bat of our love, Sir
Autograph it in the shining ink
Of your courage, truthfulness
Deep wisdom and composure
Get into the Indian crease and hit
Sixes into our skies and beyond

Please do proud
Of the great land of the Ganges
We are out on the grounds
Holding the tricolor
Under the vast Indian skies
To run with you our torch-bearer
And celebrate your triumphs
The breeze and winds will follow
As we together make our morrow
Breathing India in unison

65. Cricket of the Stars

Today
Two giant nations are to meet
Eyeball to eyeball
On a foreign ground

Media made big business out of it
They called it the Clash Of The Titans
The steely determination of India
That shames the plants of Jamshedpur
And the ferocious black might of the Indies
Running amok rampaging
In a run-hunt spree

Astrologers made hay
While the Sun of the zodiac shone
His way along the heavens
They had predictions even
Of the exact runs each side would make
No matter if they erred
Who would remember
When the fight was over

People of the two nations
Nay of the whole world
Sat pinned to their televisions
Forgetting their roles
As father, mother, son, daughter
What a tragedy
If a game hijacks
Human felicity
And if a hungry child cries
Deprived of its usual dose of milk

The steel came first
Rigid as he should be
And ducked his way back to pavilion
The black titan roared
Made four and that was the end
He ran back to where he came from
No matter what records he had broken

And everyone who witnessed the scene
Said it was all in the stars
And that consoled the astrologers
Who had their maths widely off mark

And then the tail-enders came
Hit the ball hither and thither
In panic, had narrow escapes
Which were attributed to human error
After all humans are to err
If the stars are the deciding factor

And at the end of the day one team won

Just on the sheer power of the tail-enders

Whoever they were no one bothers

Don't ask me the name of the winning team

If it was all in the heavens

Why don't you ask the stars

They are there gaping at you night long

In a stupor of indifference that to you rightly belong

When you play the game of the great Lord

As though you are at London's Lord's

66. A Nation Called India

As I sat to watch
The TV after a long grind at my desk
One channel discussed
Why Sonia did what she did
Quoting her erstwhile loyal aides

Another went to Gaza
Debated the torment
Palestinians underwent
Chided Israel for being criminally adamant

Yet another one claimed
An ISI spy had designs
Planned from his base in Sri Lanka
To bomb vital sites in South India

Those who participated in the debates
Had mouthfuls to speak
In a wild cacophony that confused
Themselves and the hosts
As the viewers dozed off
Indifferent to their nation's turmoil

As my sisters, daughters and mothers
Across a land called India
Got disrobed and wailed in pain
In a manner one of their great epics said
God knows what parts of their bodies bled

Who cares?
Don't ask me please
I am too indifferent
I am an Indian to the hilt
My comfort lies in sleep

67. Woman

They said
You are my better half
Out of my rib you came
Bullshit, I say
You are the whole
You have never been half

Throw Adam to the winds
Eve was always full
All this talk about half and quarter
Coming off a rib whatever
Is just childish prattle
A woman is always full
As green as mother earth and lushly filled

My mom was full
A full woman all the while
No matter what my silly dad thought
No matter how many times she wept
Who would care what he felt
In his chauvinistic masculinity
That had no meaning
Beyond the hairs of his silly moustache
That greyed and died in time

We belong to a land
Where Mother reigns supreme
She stomps the heavens
As well as the earth below
She is the power
That creates the worlds
We call Her by a million names
And yet never are we satisfied

Woman, woman, woman
Mother, mother, mother
Get into the veins of men
Be their life-blood so
There always is a flow
Unto infinity
Unending procreativity

Oh woman, what is the world
Without you and your smile
Here are the flowers that I can find
From all over the earth
At your feet, never ever fret
Men know they can't be
Without you on their left

Fools are they
Just forgive
For you are woman
You always forgive

68. Lotus Land

India is a lotus land,
In full bloom, all white and red.
We begin our days
Saluting the Lord of the Day,
Who rises holding a white lotus
On a chariot of seven horses.

Our Goddesses of Word and Wealth
Are seated on lotuses,
One white and the other red
Oh, ours is land of lotuses.

We thump our chest
And say "I, I, I am the best",
Our Sage says:
"That "I" is not you,
Look underneath
What you thump,
There is a lotus,
Lotus of the heart,
Your sacred retreat,
The divine habitat.".

India is a lotus land,
In full bloom, all white and red.
I was a boy in teens
In my native Kerala,
A land full of ponds,
Who once swam a silver pool
In the early morning sun
To pluck a lotus
For his blushful girlfriend.

His feet got caught
In the mesh underneath,
In the netty knottiness
Of intricate roots.
He struggled hard to extricate
Himself in anguish and panic.

For the first time in life
Fear of death he tasted.
Lotuses all around
Looked and smiled,
They gave him hope
And enthused him to fight.

When at last the Lord
Helped him back to land
To hand the flower to the anxious lass,
He saw bees in her lashes
Hovering over red lotuses -
Her blushful cheeks,
And forgot all about
The struggle just bygone

Swinging to and fro,
Between pain and smile,
He grew up to learn
About the six circles
Of the Kundalini.
Each one was a lotus again
Of different number of petals,
The last one on the crown
In full bloom with thousand leaves
Where his Ma resides
As his resplendent Self.

And when he slept
He knew he was a pond
Of countless lotuses,
In full bloom, all white and red -
A body of shining water
With blossoms smiling all over.

Oh India is a lotus land,
In full bloom, all white and red,
Listening to the lullaby of the stars.

69. My First Love Letter

It was when I was just in class three
Hovering around the tenth year of age
Something bothered me in the hours wee
A sweetness, an aroma, sweat
Or was it the morning dew on grass
That kept me awake
Rolling on my smelly bed
With a sweetness that blazed my glands

I don't know, I can't tell
But there was she
My classmate
With jasmine teeth
A dance perched on her feet
Bothering my budding masculinity

I knew I wanted her
I couldn't make out what for
In a frenzy that engulfed me
Like a forest fire then I wrote
On the inside of a discarded cigarette pack
Slit open like a bleeding heart
What I felt, the first love letter
In words that moved like ants
All over me and my heart

I handed it to her brother
Two years younger
In secret, behind the school toilet yonder
Hoping it would reach and vanquish her

But, there was the maths teacher
Fondling his scorpion tail moustache
Watching the goings-on
Who intercepted the missive
From the hands of the shivering brother

I thought I was in for hell
Punishment, beatings, no one can tell
But nothing happened to my surprise
Till at last I noticed
The school headmistress at my fence
In a rare bosom chat with my mom, her friend

I was playing behind my house
Rolling stones in the setting sun
Like a forlorn Ulysses adorned in sweat
Yet I knew I was their subject

Days passed and Diwali came
The Indian festival of lights
It was time for the early morning bath
Under the glistening stars
My mom poured warm water over me from a tub
And I misbehaved in a gleeful jump
She cautioned and slapped me on my thigh
With a fire unknown in her eyes
"Idiot, have you begun
Writing love letters at this age? "

That was the first and last time
She ever beat me
A lovely mother was she
And, often I wonder what happened
To that passionate missive of mine

Perhaps, it was blown over by the winds
Over fences and thorns and profusely bled
And withered in the sun and rain
Decayed down the channels of time

And I met her of late one of these days
At a temple festival when I braved
To tell her about my missive missed
That perhaps could have changed our fate

She laughed out in a guffaw
An aging grandma of three
And I could see at sixty-eight
Her jasmines were still intact
What more could a lover want
When he has only a toothless smile
In exchange, Oh, why do we age?

70. Anyone Out There?

He made man in His image
The Book said
Man defined life
To his liking
Made it mandatory
Water should exist
For intelligence to sustain

He stood gasping
Looking at the heavens
Am I alone here?
Is anyone out there?

The stars as always
Looked down upon him
The ignorant fool
With their shimmering gaze
In utter unconcern
Who thought on borrowed intelligence
And yet prided
He owned and knew everything
The master of the universe

And now his research has found

A planet somewhere

In the wilderness of the skies

A body of matter exists

With an abundance of water on it

Possibility of a companion on it

He got out of his bath-tub naked

Shouted to the world

Eureka, Eureka! I have found

A habitat in the universe

That can house

An image of mine

Life on earth

Watered by the very water

That I drink

That I offer to the Lord

In my morning prayers

And in Holy Communion

Across the world

I am not alone

Never have I been

A being more intelligent

Who breathed acid fumes

Took his daily bath

In acid ponds

Laughed at the mundane fool

Holding aloft a toast

Of cheers with his acid drink

A mountain inert
Right beside him
Pitied how far ignorance could go
This guy with the telescope
Knows everything
Yet he fails
To read the pulsating heart
Of the very thing next to him
That he considers lifeless
And prefers to philander
In ignorance of the sublimest kind

Never has anyone here been alone
When the Lord is constant companion
And who that Lord never ever ask
When the asking is a borrowed task

71. Kitchen of Abundance

Aroma of dosas being cooked
Chutney being garnished
Asafoetida boiling in the sambar mix
All emanate from my neighborhood
As I take my early morning strolls
Around our apartment complex

Unseen by me there is
A mother eager to pack lunch
For her son rushing for the six-thirty local
A wife her hair wrapped in towel
Still wet from bath
Filling her husband's lunch box
With warmth and care

A child with slumberous eyes
Languorous yawns
Watching them hurry
Unwilling to get up and start
The daily morning chores
Mandatory before his school starts

Blessed are the households
Where the woman is taken for granted
The food is ready
With the aroma of life and love in it

A bachelor here I am
With no culinary skill
In the kitchen of abundance
Ruled by the unseen Mother
Roofed by the stars
Fumbling with unfamiliar utensils

Smelling the scent of food
The aroma of love and sweat
That permeates my neighborhood
Knowing for sure
That my steaming plate
Would be ready for me to devour
Around the turn of the hour

I don't worry how it comes
For I am so sure
My Mother wouldn't ever fail
Her unknowing ignorant son
For she is nothing but
So very much the sweating love itself

72. Jesus on the Cross

Last night, I had a dream
I was self-realized

The 'I' that writes this
Didn't exist then
Like Jesus on the Cross

The Cross is me
My torturers are me
The hurt is me
Then how can this pain of nails
Biting into 'my' flesh ever hurt me
For am I not ever the nails
The blood and the pain?

Outside on the horizon
A Christmas sun is drowning
Itself into reddish inebriation
So let the exhilarated hand type on
Whatever it can
Before the dark
Pushes it forever down
Into unknown oblivion

73. Shoddy Bar

They sat facing one another
Inside the shoddy bar
Swarthy figures
Like in American cartoons
Their visages waxen
Looks distant
Cadaverous blank

The figures of Jesus On The Cross
His pain lighted
By a low watt crimson bulb
Smiling Lord Ganesh
Granting boons
With burnt-out incense sticks
Before him
Presided over the scene

Each had a burden
Perhaps the dejection
Due to cruel rejection
Of the past to bury
Or a long-lost love
A broken wedlock
Death of a sweet-heart
A broken heart of some sort

They sat
Puffing at their fags
Or beedis
Or whatever they had
The glow at the tip
Of what they smoked
Said it all
The burn that rued their hearts

Aches of the like
The winds of the plains
Could hardly hope to soothe
Angst, the wisdom
Of the silent mounts around
Could ever undo

They sat puffing and drinking
In silence at the cacophonous bar
Shoddy, dilapidated
Infested with flies
Flying insects and mice

Dreaming they could once again
Sit with their kids
Under hurricane lamps
Late into the night
Helping them with their lessons
As the clouds rumbled
On distant mountain tops

As their wives garnished
Some favourite dish
In smoky kitchens unlit
Wiping burning eyes
With greying sari tips

Later to return
To their late night beds
To grant midnight warmth
Of sweat and love
That made the nights
More odoriferous
Than the incense burnt
Before indifferent Gods

They longed and longed
As every drink sank
Into their burning core
To return to the shores of love afar
As the world outside brimmed
Calling them drunkards

Refusing to grant
There are addictions of sorts
Religion, power and fads
Women, avarice, greed
That ruined humankind
More than the drinks
The entire humanity drank

With their glasses emptied
They would now decamp
Like moths fleeing a dying lamp
Into the night's waiting arms
To the big bar under the shimmering stars
Where the cups are full again
With tears frothing in grief and pain

Where they would lie wide awake
After a fitful nap past midnight
On their unkempt beds like dried-up twigs
To roll and roll alone in pain
Sob and cry again in vain
And sing to far off receding plains
Where their solace hidden, remains

74. I Am a Butterfly!

I was a butterfly
That knew not the Sun
Who showed me this and that
In whose dazzle I lost the sight
Of the One that shone in all

My eyes were closed
As I drowned
In the sweetness that nectar bore
Thought that was all
There to be known

Alas, I was a butterfly
Inebriate dumb and deaf
That moved and died in time
Like leaves on autumn eve

Till I landed on the beads
Clung to them in mortal grief
The lute and lotus then I saw
With the One who sat on it
Whose Lotus Feet said it all

I am a butterfly
Who now sees the Sun
In whose light shines one and all
I am a butterfly
Who knows where
Sweet immortality rears

The lute is me
The flower is me
As the Mother who smiles
And shines around

I am a butterfly
That knows no fret
For fret I am, the Feet I am
The sweetness too I am
I am a butterfly
Lost in Love
That sees only butterflies around
And that Oneness - the seat of all!

75. The Eternal Romantic

When I was young
Bloody hot-blooded
I fancied there could be
An eternal kiss
In an endless embrace

Then they called me
An indefatigable romantic

Later when my beard greyed
I knew eternal anything can't be
Everything that had begun
Had to end in vain
In vagrant time on endless run

Then they called me
A sophic akin to Socrates

Ah me, they didn't know
I remained still a romantic
For then I was in love
Not with fleshy lips alone
But with roaches even

I am a romantic
Endless that I am
Holding everything
Kiss, roach, touch and lips
Close to my chest
In an eternal clasp

76. Dubai

Dubai
The mushroom city
Of time in fast motion

Dubai
A dreamer's extravaganza
On man's unquenchable ambition

Dubai
Yesterday's barren expanse
Now a mirage growing unto heaven

A kaleidoscopic phantasmagoria
Of colours, glitter, light
Pomp, speed and wealth
All mounted together
On a speeding roller-coaster

Life a mere spectator
Standing aside unsure
An unwitting witness
Lame, insecure on its crutches

The play goes on and on
Ephemeral, transient
Spread all over, iridescent
On a boundless billboard
Eternal, impersonal

77. Dussehra

Men, women and children
Sat everywhere in the brilliant sun
Selling red and yellow flowers
Incense, sugar-cane, puffed rice, sweets
In the vicinity of the Durga temple
Right on the road
Obstructing traffic
Unmindful of somnambulistic passersby

Walkers walked the roads
As though in a dream
Their demeanour astral
Motorists stopped right
In the middle of the road
Before the temple
To say their prayers
Caring two hoots
For the noisy hoots
Of impatient honkers behind
They had a sign on their hind glass
"If you honk, you are a retard"

The time is Dussehra in India
When the Universal Mother descends
To stomp the streets
In victorious valour
On the back of Her ferocious lion
When not having
Dangerously trespasses
Into the territory of
Over-abundance

Street dogs fought in abandon
Perhaps inspired
By Her unseen presence
No one cared
Rabies was the last thing
Anyone feared
When the Mother was around
To bless everyone with Her looks
That warded off plague and pox

Women with jasmine
Loaded on their black oiled hair
Breezed around in chatter
Like spring clouds
Those who discerned saw the Mother
In them and bowed in reverence
Their sweat smelt the Mother
On poor earth
What more can any man care?

A solitary cumulonimbus
Laboured on the hills
Watching the scene
Undecided if she should rain
Her bowels filled with
Thunder, fire and lightning
Like the hungry ones on the ground

Awareness stood witness
Capturing the scene
The Mother of everything
Born, unborn and dying

I lay before Her prostrating
My incapable arms clasping
The neck of Her Lion and mane
Where else can a poor Indian soul
Find its peace than at Her feet?
Bless us Mother with your looks
A multitude of ignorant fools
Bacterial on the streets of life

78. Indian Motherhood

A working mother of South India
Rushed into a speeding local bus
As a Coimbatore afternoon
Slanted its way to death
On an impersonal mountain-top
Of the uncaring Western Ghats

She had to reach home
Make tea for her man
Back from business
God knows what
And out of bed
After an afternoon snooze
With blood-shot eyes
And yelling kids bespectacled
Just back from school
Hooked to the TV screens
Watching meaningless comics

The bus sped past
Many a speeding stop
Where forlorn puppies wailed
For their mothers barbecued
On fuming tar
Where abandoned mothers begged
For food and alms
Their distraught eyes and stomachs
Afire like the summer sun

The mother had to reach
Her home neverthelsss
Make tea for eyes
Blood-shot or bespectacled
Tucking in her sari pleats

Perspiring all the time
Shaming Arabian perfume
That is Indian womanhood
Pause and salute her silent toil
The unfailing aroma of her sweat

79. Prayer

Someone once complained
He was in real bad straits
I asked him if he prayed
He said he did day and night

Poor guy was secure
But he was not sure
A prisoner of expectations
A seeker after inexhaustible wants

To have the will and time
To sit and pray is a boon
With grace granted by Heavens
Know you unthinking ones

Good times have begun
If in prayer you get drowned
The day you forget surrender
Know for sure you are asunder

80. Freedom from What?

The British ruled us Indians
We wanted freedom
It was given but then
Hot-heads who looked
Towards the Soviets
And then to Mao said

That is not enough
We need freedom
From oppression
Don't you see the exploitation
Of the downtrodden
The sweating unfortunate
The milling proletariat?

We went to the jungles
Learnt guerrilla tactics
Adored heroes
Who had died fighting
In distant Bolivia, Cuba
And Latin America

We despised the West
Thought they were the pest
Adorned gore on our face
Didn't matter who that we killed
As long as it was freedom
That we thought we fought for
Till we realized
The fight never had an end

Then came a wise man my way
Wise because he had a beard
Asked me what was it from which
I needed myself to be free

With a drink raised in my hand
My eyes myopic
I told him I wanted all that
That would let me and the world live
Free from economic grief

He said my wish was granted
I walked a strident gait
My bag full of wealth
That made Bill Gates jealous

Then I shuddered
There was one second to me
'Yon Cassius, he has a hungry look'
He would any moment
Strangle my neck
And be the number one
In this nasty money game

I spent sleepless nights
When at last the bearded guy
Appeared before me and asked
What was it that
I needed then
My long-lasting freedom from

I forgot Cassius
For I knew he would go my unhappy way
Answered I feared death
I would have me wisdom unfetter
From the fear of dying forever

The cunning bearded sage
Said it was done
I was then ninety
Sagging on a stick
An anachronism of flesh and bones
That communicated with none
With no contemporaries around
To share my teeming thoughts

What would be my state
If I hit two hundred without death
A wrinkled mass worse
Than the famed Rip Wan Winkle
All alone in a world
Where I didn't actually belong?

Freedom from death
Then was not
My want, what was freedom
If my habit is want?
Wanting idiot I am
How is that I can
Rid me off the desire for want?

The grey of the beard
Laughed and said
All that you need
Is freedom from want
It is granted
'Here you look,
Life is a sojourn, know you not
How you began, how you will end,
Or, if you began and will end at all,
All are just a given
Granted by whom know we not'

'Live in peace why you don't
Without wants accept
With your head ever bent
To whoever the one keeps giving on
Aren't you then free,
Aren't you then the freedom sought? '

'Aren't you then the stars
The breeze, rain and sky
All that crawl and all that fly
What is the freedom that you seek
If you are freedom ever-free
Unbound by horizons, the illusory sky? '

81. Assadoo (Weaving Art of Arabian Gulf)

The desert lies dreaming
As an Arabian night ages
Vagrant winds wander
Aimless on the sands
Drawing patterns intricate -
Nature's sublime assadoo

*Men clad in bishts**
Languish in summer tents
Feeling important
Heavily perfumed
Waving rosaries
Their eyes glittering
*Mystified by sheesha** fumes*
Nurturing unknown dreams -
Secrets of sublime assadoo

*A buxom beauty in burqa****
Her hand shading her eyes
An envy for mascara
Waiting at the door-steps
For her man to return
From a distant errand
Tired on camel back
Silhouetted against the sun
A big orange that sinks -
Dusk's sublime assadoo

Children scampering up and down
The ephemeral dunes
In the golden evening sun
Noisy as they hail
The distant water cart
Inching towards the village heart
From the far off end of land -
Life's beautiful assadoo

The mind returns to its hearth,
*The great 'bayth assadoo' *****
Where the dark windy nights,
Dust, sun and cold,
Camel hooves on sand,
Rugged men holding falcons,
Damsels in chatter,
Kids with matted hair
Holding their mothers' attire,
All mingle on a weaving wheel
In a wonderful assadoo

The night-sky smiles down on the huts
As moonlight spreads across
The starry expanse above
Grace of God's great assadoo

———

** A gilded ornamental drape worn by men over their dress on special occasions*

*** Water-pipe hookah (hubble-bubble)*

**** Loose black enveloping garment worn by Muslim women*

***** House of assadoo - name of a museum in Kuwait where assadoo artefacts are on display*

82. Haiku Calendar

January arrives
Winter sun with golden rays
Scribbles greeting cards

Maid February
Takes out little kids to play
Group of golden clouds

Mountain fires aglow
March awake worried about
Coming summer heat

Sun is April smith
Melts gold and shapes ornaments
For seasons to wear

Lonely rain bird sings
Summer clouds pour at midnight
With May fireworks grand

South-west monsoon clouds
Scurry fast across the sky
June listens for rain

It rains a deluge
Frogs play night-long orchestra
July fast asleep

Rain takes holiday
It is Independence Day
August's tricolor

Flower processions
Colour September landscape
Harvest festival

October thunders
Evening downpours deluge
North-East Monsoon in

November star kids
Peep from under a blanket
Chilly new moon night

Venus leads the stars
Carols along zodiac
December choir

83. Sunanda Pushkar

*(An obituary to Sunanda, politician Shashi Tharoor's wife, who was found dead in
a Delhi hotel room.)*

Sunanda

We never met

We never knew each other

You were just a charming presence

An ebullient efflorescence

That off and on graced our TV screens

You crashed into my awareness

When your wedding news

With a handsome politician

An unlikely combination

Who had run up to the top of the UN

Human form of linguistic eloquence

Hailing from my own town

Who tweeted faster than the morning birds

Hit the headlines

And blazed our channels

Later, I saw you
Chasing his frenetic perambulations
At parties and events
Your sunny smile
Always made sure
His shadow cast no darkness

Sunanda
I sat up at the news
That you have gone
Forever, stunned
A lady has gone
Not a politician's consort
But a gracious presence
A woman made of romance
And the stuff of dreams
From our noisy midst

Sunanda
They will talk and talk
Weave new stories
Sensationalize your exit
Dissect and analyze
Your past, what you did and didn't
Conjecture possibilities
About what really happened
To satisfy rumour mills
As the doctors would
On your frail lifeless corpus

You were a fluttering butterfly
That died in the morning dew
Rest in peace, Oh, grace
A tear-drop here I place
Beside you where you lie
Dripping from a wrenching heart
An utter stranger's tribute
For we can only cry
When those of dream-stuff die

84. Philosophy of a House Cat

(Inspired by my eldest brother's cat, Patches, in Durham, North Carolina)

I am a house cat
I live in me
I am I am
Always I am
Meow meow

This house is my world
Perfect in itself
With what is not here
Never am I concerned
Content with myself
Happily disposed

I am not alone
When my master is out
I move about meowing
Rubbing against things
My friends in the house
Brooding saints

He comes and goes
His movements are unknown
Makes always sure
My bowl has good measure
He knows my likes
What I should take
I have no complaints
Nothing that aches

Fridge in the kitchen
Hums a tune
Untiring singer
Never asleep
Wind on the panes
Call me out
Swaying the woods
I shan't be seduced
Legs of the table
Sage-like stoics
Always mum
I nudge them for fun

I have a lot
To talk to them
So do I meow
And move about

My master's movements
Aren't my worry
I am content
Least uncertain
The keyhole will sound
To raise my ears
And he will enter
Fast in a hurry

To return my meows
And stroke my head
To clean my potty
And call me naughty

My tail will be raised
My back will peak
To rub his legs
And rest by his side
My eyelids closed
Immersed in me
As he broods
Reads his books

Often we sit
Watching the TV
Together for long
In deep reverie
Untouched by glitter
Tears and laughter
Lost in ourselves
One in one

There is my ilk
Out in the woods
Strayed into wrongs
Fighting it out
Running about
Dying in hordes
My ears are closed
To their noisy calls
I hold my calm
I am I am
Always I am

World the temptress
Calls through the glass
Pines, oaks and cedars
Swing in the winds
Shaking their heads
Shiver in cold
Drenched in rain
Fall in storms
A place of change
Birth and death
A tragic mess
Where I don't belong

Swarms of moth
Dance in sunlight
As they fly
Over the bushes
Flashy delights
That don't remain
No lasting pleasure
I am not swayed

The world of men
Beyond the woods
Crashes in booms
And bangs aloud
A deluded lot
As they screech
Along the roads
Of ego-driven life
To pangs and pains
Hopelessly maimed

I live in me
I am I am
In my master's sanctuary
I am I am
Always I am
Morrow is never my worry
Be a house cat
In the Master's hall
Grieve you not ever shall

85. East Wind

Someone said
The East wind began blowing last night
I didn't know, I was fast asleep

The coconut palms looked westward
When I awoke
The palmyras on the plains
Sang a vibrant song
Which I knew from childhood
That spoke of grandma fairy-tales
Kerosene lamps casting shadows on the walls
Kids listening with gleaming eyes
Before they retired to their smelly beds
Far away the wail
Of lonely trains on insolent rails

The East wind had in fact begun at midnight
Without my knowledge, I was asleep
Bringing in scents of incense burnt
At temples in the East
Their spires kissing the skies
Of champak, jasmine and tulsi leaves
Camphor fumes and sound of bells
Of a Dravidian past of yore
The mirth of waves afar
In the Bay of Bengal
Across the Palghat Pass
Where I live
Walled by the Western Ghats
On the South and North

Oh East wind, send me the silver clouds
Your children, to the kindergarten on the mounts
Where they would dance without cease
All day long and I would watch
With glee, my day already made

86. Silk Routes

Silk routes of India converged
On the South Indian city of Cochin
Where brides demurred and glittered
At a sprawling sari arcade
Like lamps on a windless Diwali night

Colors poured over them
As did unwed salesgirls
Attending on and draping them with passion
Their hearts filled with dreams
Of rainbow hues
Of eligible men on the distant horizon
With wedding garlands in their hands

The sale should go on
Season or no season
Monsoon or no rain
No matter who weds or remains unwed
Insensitive remains
Silk and fiber to youthful dreams
Heart, emotions and passion

Delighted stood the prospective bride

A smile perched on her lips

Busy moved the salesgirls around like bees

With a Goddess sobbing in their hearts

Silent like the unwed one of the Cape

Lighted by a flickering lamp on a summer night

As silk routes converged on Cochin

Careless who did wed or who did weep

87. The Jujube Tree and Me

We saw every evening
And greeted each other
The jujube tree and me
In the middle of the desert
Where I took my evening strolls

Ours was a friendship
That needed no introduction
For we knew without knowing
We were in each other
From time immemorial
In creation endlessly eternal
Yet never ever begun
Like the star and the sky
The moon and the rabbit on her lap

She grew on barren land
Perhaps from a vagrant bird drop
Giving existence
Luxuriant expression
In her ever-verdant radiance

When the desert decides to smile
Aren't tropical paradises often shamed?
Her foliage had all the green
And shine nature could ever glean

★ 257 ★

Children wandering the desert
Ravaged her leaves
For the gems she bore
In magnanimous abundance
At the close of winter months
Yet she never complained

She watched them play
In her secure shade
Like a mother in snooze
Half alert and half dazed
While the afternoons slothfully aged

Birds thronged her branches
Made nests and brooded
Imparting warmth to their eggs
In wintry nights
Looking at the stars
Their little heads filled
With the mirth of moonlit nights

Alas! I didn't find her in her place
This evening with a beaming smile
What all that remained
Was an upturned stump
A clump of broken roots
That called out in vain
To a sinking evening sun
Like the raised hands of the dead
In a massacre scene

She has been felled
And unceremoniously carted
Away to give way
To a prestigious monument
To be made of concrete
Glazed tiles and marble
That would commemorate
An achievement
In preserving environment

A pain grips my heart
Like an angina in rage
As I sink on my knees
To touch those dying hands
Of my departed mate
Distressed like the birds
Homeless and wailing
Brittle eggs crushed
Embryos whimpering in sunshine

I raise my eyes
Tearfully refracted
To an elusive horizon
Blurred and distant
Saintly impersonal
As the summer wind whispers

The tree and you are destined
To meet again and again
In an unending sojourn
To share your tears and pain
And perish in vain
Periodically vandalized
By space and time

What it matters if a mate
Is missed for a while
When she is inseparable
And eternally in you -
The jujube tree and you

88. To Death

I lay unconscious
For a fortnight
Throwing my entrails out
On a forlorn hospital bed
Down with enteric fever

All that I remember hearing then
Through slits
Of my sinking awareness
Were the North East January winds
Violently rustling the banyan trees

I never feared you then
You didn't matter to me
For I was primitive
In my still nascent innocence

I survived and grew up
Later to be poetic
I was worried
I would lose the beauty
Of the east winds
And the Monsoon rains
If you pounced on me unwawares

I spent sleepless nights
Rolled on my bed
Feared you were there
In the dark
Outside my hut
With a noose
To squeeze my fragile neck

Idiot I was
Till I knew
That I knew you
That you were always with me
Nibbling at my corpus
That isn't really me
Like a rat
Inching towards its last savored gulp

What does it matter rat
You have always been there
To feast on what I mistook I was?
You always needed me
To acknowledge and validate
Your own flimsy existence
A silly mongrel you are
Tamed to the very hilt
The next time your food is ready
I will call you, till then wait

My backyard is your home
As it is
For the mango tree
Mewing cat, the evening sky
I will ever remain
Lighting your eccentricities
And absurdities
To the ignorant world around me
Wait and pant
That is all
What you are supposed to do
Till I have another errand for you

89. As I Lay Embryo-like

The scope went down the food pipe
Lighting its contracting walls
Down to a frothing stomach
Where they scratched out
A piece of suspected tissue
To look at it later at leisure
And ascertain the secrets of its texture.

I lay embryo-like
Folding my hands around my head
In prostration to the might of science
A toy in the hands of bespectacled intelligence
Pouring over me in profound seriousness.

I lay embryo-like
Sedated in primal state
As my entrails curled up
Like earthworms in the sun
To their curious prodding.

Another tube headed up the colon
To pinch a piece
Of an innocent polyp
That swayed its head
Like hyacinth in the wind.
Blood splashed around bright
Painted the flesh Picasso-like.

They would look at the bit later again
Under their scopes
In air-conditioned labs
And nod their heads
In grave silence.
God only knows what that would mean.
Or, who would care?
I could only think embryo-like
Sedated into my primal state.

The tubes scoured me up and down,
They thought they knew me too well now,
To fill their talks at lunch
What each cell, each hole, each bit
Of my pulsating corpus meant.

Yet I lay sedate, unknown to them
Like a sunken sun behind the crimson hill
Radiating into trees, winds and sky
And the last chirps of homing birds,
Housing a universe in my heart.

They thought they knew me too well

As they peered into every cell

For foreboding changes that spelt hell.

Yet, they knew me not

The one who lay sedate

Worlds away from them

Holding the universe in his fondly clasp.

90. 61 Clinic Road

I stood shivering, teeth chattering
In the bitter winter cold
Before the monstrous mall
That sucked men, women and kids in
Like Medusa with her tentacles fanning

It was my maiden visit to the city
Of my teenage dreams
Famed for its gardens
Spacious parks and spots of fun

My old flame once lived here
Her parents had ripped her
Off from me and my village
At a time we had thought
Nothing could ever make us part
Leaving me bleeding like a shrub
From which a red-rose had just been plucked

It was a December eve
Crowds braved the chill
To welcome New Year
My wife just went into the mall
Leaving me, her bodyguard,
On sentry's job
Outside on the road
It would be eons
Before she returned
Lots of time to stand and yawn

It was then that I read
To the left where I stood
The name of the road
"Clinic Road" in bold
On a worn-out rust-eaten blue board

It took me on time-travel
Forty-five years into the past on a glider
To my village post office
Where I waited impatient
For the postman to sort the mail
And hand me precious letters from out of his heap
Arriving from this distant town
To be exact
House 61 on Clinic Road

The missives of passion
Always smelt of her sweat
Aroma of her breath
Carried her anxious sobs
Silken fabric of her dreams

Often soaked in tears
They mingled with my village winds
Summer rains and paddy fields
Waxing moon and starry skies
Drunken of her words then I walked
As though on the Milky Way
With the sweetest ache ever in my heart

Curious I moved towards the mall
To ask a vendor where 61 stood
I told him it was a house
Where a dear one of mine once homed

He looked at me in disbelief
"House! ? " he exclaimed
"Uncle, look, this mall here
Is number 61 since the day I came
And that was thirty years into the past"

"Oh, yea, I had heard when I was a child
Some small houses had stood this side
Surrounded by shrubs and trees
They had roofs made of asbestos
On which crazy rains played crescendo"

"A group from Mumbai razed the place
To build here this magnificent arcade
The pride of the city the like of which
There are hardly two or three
Across the breadth and width of the country"

At some point coordinated by space and time
A girl here sat deep into the night
To pour her heart on paper
And that 'here' is not anymore
Forever it has disappeared

My heart sank at the news
As I realized with a shudder
All that remained was non-real
Which fools christen "here and there".

Yet, in vain, my yearning heart
Longed again for the long-lost past
To feel at close the warmth of her breath
Starry eyes and deep-drawn sighs
As she paused and wrote her words
Filled with the passion of autumn nights

Perhaps a smiling waxing moon
Slanted over her little house
Imparting the scene the charm of a dream
Perhaps she saw a lonely star
Outside her window on a swaying palm
Smiled and prayed in supplication
To express in right words her emotions

That scene has vanished without a trace
Vandalized by space and time
Which have conspired in cahoots
To raise a mall in its place
Absurd, monstrous, out of place
Inert, wanton, concretized

The girl has disappeared into the folds of time
Yet, why are her old words and dreams
Left behind in endless streams
For a shivering heart to receive and ache
In a cold windless December night?
Tell me, please, wise bearded souls:
Why this ache and who aches?
What is it that aches?
And who is it that is ached?
And why doesn't wisdom undo the ache?

91. Guide Me Light

Bearded wise
I had faith
In them so I listened
As they explained
Scripture and wisdom
In different ways

They have now let me down
En masse they have moved
To counter proselytization
To be one-up-man
In the number game of conversion
And reconversion
Where they counted only sheep-heads
And not the stuff in the heads
Falling prey to proselytization

Basking in the glory of an ancient past
When planes adorned with flowers
Flew unmemorable skies
Shaming recent Bernoulli
When they knew the velocity of light
To the last decimal point
Making Einstein and others shady borrowers
Of knowledge that existed
Just between the icy mounts on the North
And Cape Comorin on the South

As pastors and priests
Supposed to be shepherds
Misled their herd
Predated among fools
To sell their message
In dubious ways
And swell their folds

As the intelligentsia of the West
Thought caricatures and cartoons
Would earn millions if they hurt
Sentiments in the name of free speech
And traded their heads in gory bloodshed

As bearded men with guns and bombs
Moved about wiping out
Humans they thought
Were their enemies
Oh, where is the olive branch?

On blood-soaked ground of despair and hate

Here I sit, I have only the Light

That shines in me, so I beseech "Guide me Light"

As ever I have done from my ancient past

A forlorn destitute betrayed

By his own wisdom

Those who teach

And the world around

92. Happy New Year

Last year
At midnight of 31st December
I lighted a lamp
Raised a toast to the stars with one hand
And a roaring Kalanishkov with the other
And cheered "HAPPY NEW YEAR"

That is my annual ritual
Since time immemorial
Since the days I committed
My first fratricides
With Cain and then with Romulus

With every New Year then
I made steady progress
Into matricide first
And then to patricide
To quench my unquenchable thirst
For power and wealth

With every kill that I made
I never missed
To tell my kids
That man is the ultimate
In the Creator's list
Different from the beasts
I slaughtered and ate

And then from my roof-top
Again with a grin and a gun in hand
Swore "I am the ultimate,
Because I am self-aware"

In the now dying old New Year
My score-card is brighter
Than ever before
For I have now
Traversed into genocide
Deeper and deeper

God now would be immensely pleased
That in His name I have this year
Killed more than ever before
In populicide and genocide
What a New Year I have made
Wiping out entire ethnicities
And firing at unwary innocents
In sacred paedicide!

Yet, again tonight
I would shamelessly light my lamp
With a gun in hand
And say Happy New Year to the stars

For I am different and ultimate
In Lord's creation that I am self-aware
And taught to hope for a future
That contrasts my actions of the past

So this time over
Let it be a real HAPPY NEW YEAR
May the lamp I light tonight
Burn brighter
In the breath of my hope
So tidings are different
And history changes course

93. Uncle Passed Away

Uncle passed away in sleep
In the wee hours today in peace
The breeze held its sibilant breath
Leaves paused and listened in depth

He was ninety-two, three-fourth blind
Yet, exuberant like a playful child
Never did he mouth a complaint
His smile never ever waned

He lived all alone in a bustling town
As his kin and children worked abroad
He never sought a helping hand
Content full with his own hands

And a maid who came once a day
To cook his food and clean the place
His mood upbeat, infectious grace
Enthralled those who saw his face

The world for him was a shadow play
Delights galore in dance and sway
As he swished and made his way
Silent like a fish in a bay

He moved in and out of his flat
His sense of touch made sure that
He was always on the right spot
With his unfading smile intact

He knew where what was placed
The right elevator button to press
Sense of touch told him well
The exact count in his wallet's swell

Uncle proved exemplary
To all his contemporaries
He was the best lesson they could have
On graceful aging sans fear of grave

Smiling on his bed he lay
Rustle and winds stilled mid-way
A white lamb stood bleating at his feet
It was death, helpless, uncle had it tricked

94. Sedona - Land of Gods

Ethereal celestial land
Of red rock mountains
Vermilion on the plains
Of Arizona's forehead

You have me seduced
Charmed and bewitched
With the golden sun
Rising and sinking
In your curvaceous folds
Like a lover in eternal thrall

Your hills are a pantheon
Of unfinished visages
Of Gods no one knows
Sculpted perhaps
By wandering aliens
Who left on some emergent errand
Across infinite galactic spans
To return some day with chisels in hand

While the clouds and winds
Bathe and wipe the gods
With unflinching devotion
Every turn of the seasons

While the humming birds
Hover and sing their praise
Beating their wings prostrate
Over paloverdes below
Their boughs all yellow
In silent veneration

While alders, ashes and sycamores
Stand motionless
Peering their ears
Yearning for the staccato
Of ancient horse-hooves
Of Apache Indians
Speeding down the slopes
For friendly rendezvous
With their ever-loving spirits

While a lonely desert quail
Unseen in a bush
Pours out her heart
Dissolving at dusk
Calling the ancient artisans to work

Sedona

You have me seduced

You are the land of gods

None other on earth can surpass

The beauty of your mounts

Oh aliens, whoever you are

Come back to this blissful land

And chisel out our future gods

95. Cactus Song

You look like a pantheon of aliens
In the dusky evening sun
At Sabino Canyon in Tucson
In holy communion
With the looming heavens

A battalion of saguaro cacti
Standing esoteric guard
At foothills and uphill
Eerie silhouettes
With hands raised
In ethereal silence
Marveling man's imagination

How much I wish I could ever remain
At these slopes after the sun has gone
To witness your silent song
To the northern constellations!

The melody that you absorb
From Mother Earth and store
In the sweet water you bear
In nectarine gallons
In your towering trunks
The song the humming bird
Finch, flicker or pecker
Taught you in silent nights
Holed up in your throbbing hearts!

Saguaros, my mystic friends
Pour out your song unabated
In silence to the Milky Way
May the earth the heavens embrace
An undying Presence we mortals sense

96. Tucson Bird

Who did build this silken nest
On this prickly mountain plant
Swaying in the vagrant winds
On this Tucson canyon ridge?

Architect of wilderness!
Am told you don't return home
Till after the sun has gone
By when canyon trips are closed

Google searches failed to tell
Who could such a home belong
You a trogon, towhee, finch
Warbler, redstart, humming bird?

With stripes on a fluffy chest
Picked from rainbows at sunset?
Do you have a crown on head
Wagging tail of golden plumes?

Are your eyes mascara-lined
Black and dark by new moon night?
Are they of a crimson tone
Shaded bright by blushful dawn?

Don't you sing like nightingales?
Do you trill and thrill the hills?
Unknown friend of earth and sky
Sweet conjecture all this mine

I can see you deep in nest
Eyes in rest with head in chest
Lighted by the lady moon
Fumbling with her starry gown

Is that so my little friend
Haven't you drunk the world too in
Starry expanse, nest and moon
Wind and night and everything?

When you sleep the world does cease
It nests in you one with you
Why does then a fool like me
Indulge in a guessing game?

Why I ponder how you look
When I too am within you
One with you and never apart
Myself am the bird you are?

Made of rapture full of song
Rainbow wings to soar aloft
To boundless freedom at last
Where time and space stand aghast

97. Poop, Poop, Poop!

I wrote a dog poem sometime back
It mentioned dogshit, know what,
someone from the enlightened West
objected to the word, as he thought
it downgraded our canine lot

The suggestion was to write poop
I dunno how that would help
As long as the thing still stinks
As bad as one can think

Well, in our gated community again
Someone found some poop this morn
On the concrete tiles of the lawn
Investigations soon began
And an expert thought aloud
It wasn't a pet's poop
But a stray one's drop

How he smelt it we know not
Yes, there is a gap in the community wall
Through which perhaps a friend had crawled
Into our domain when nature called
Manners then didn't matter at all

I believe I had a fleeting glance
Of this stray friend of ours two days back
It is a she, if I am right, and indeed a beauty
As all Indian dogs are famed to be
Whose eyes are mostly mascara-lined
Where else in the world so lovely canines be
A contrast to hairy creatures known as puppies,
Beastly dobermans, punks and the like

Oh how much I wish
Any pet lover from our midst
Adopted this beauty
So she has an official trusty
To pick and dispose of her poopy
God bless our stray dog community!

98. Hang Him After His Death

A master-mind is in our net
A bomb-maker right from birth
Set for him a special diet
The docs have advised special care
Till we hang him after his death
Jai Hind!

99. Pet Dog

A new neighbour has just moved
into our gated community.
His daughter who has delightful eyes
is all eager to keep a pet dog for her joy.

Poor fellow is worried
about the responsibilities
the possession will bring in -
walking the pet every day,
picking its smelly shit.

He is a dog domesticated by default
into a world
where he doesn't know
whose bidding he is following.

Oh Lord, bless him all the way!

100. Given

My grandson asked me:
"What blessing would you seek
this morning?"
I was washing the dishes
of the previous night
without any wishes.
I sought, therefore, to continue as I was.

"Wash the dishes?" he laughed,
asked me to bend,
placed his hand on my head
and solemnly said, "So be it".

What else could a man
nearing eighty want,
in his frail diabetic frame,
still able to move about
and watch beautiful sunsets?

Isn't life great
with the hills outside
basking in ethereal sunshine?
Isn't it a blessing
to listen to birds
singing melodious strains?

Stroke the plants and talk to them,
walk in rain, listen to streams,
all for free, look at the sky
leaning on a wayside tree,
knowing everything here
is a big 'given', well provided,
when wants are short
and the ego is laid to rest.

And who then worries
about the last breath
when the corporeal mass
that heaves sans rest
is a boon 'given'
that just comes by
without asking
on an unending sojourn?

101. Merry Christmas!

The world sings Your praise
Says You were born in a stable
To where a bright star showed the way
To wanderers of the desert

They sing carols and make new ones
Year after year every Christmas
All that is nice and sweet to hear
But Lord I have another reason
To sing out aloud
The greatness of Yours

I am no Christian by birth
Neither have I lent my ears
To missionaries who preach
And invite the world to their feuding folds

My country had a leader
Whom Your life influenced
And he put what he knew of You into practice
To free us from perilous bondage
Made us truly recognize
How You chimed with our ancient nascence

He is the Father Of Our Nation
None else in the world I think
Had the strong conviction he had
That Your teachings can be PRACTISED

My country therefore owes a lot
To You, Jesus Christ,
And to You we truly belong

Oh, guide us Divine Light
And illumine the world
Let us celebrate Christmas
To usher in an era of peace
In which the whole creation can rejoice
Unbound, without fetters and barriers
In the bosom of true Christ Consciousness
Undifferentiated Oneness

102. Petroglyphs

Petroglyphs scattered
All over Hawaii
Carved on black volcanic rocks

Mysterious they are
Stoke human curiosity
Unendingly

Human and other forms
Numbers and writings
Carved by the island's ancient natives
Long before the Whites entered the scene

No one can gauge
What they truly meant
We are left with guesses and conjectures
Lots of touristic balderdash

Me, a frail, wavering human frame
At late seventies
Walked across the blackness
On cracked volcanic lava rocks
Braving winds and sun

The past bloomed
In different forms
Carved on solidified lava
A human form here
Elsewhere a human thought
In an unknown alphabet
Or a secret number or sign

Splendorous indeed
Are the stone writings
Showcased across the island
A tourist's paradise

They dragged me back to my teenage
When I climbed a rocky peak
Close to my village home
Laboured hard on its head
And chiselled my name
Alongside my heartthrob's
My name and hers
Set apart by a heart
Pierced by an arrow
In the middle
Sweet, bleeding, passionate

Perhaps, the monsoon rains,

Winds and sunshine

Have undone my petroglyph

What else can I expect

In more than sixty years

Of my residence elsewhere

Away from my native nest

How much I wish

I could again climb that peak

To view my sweetest script

On its unthinking pate

Alas! Am now close to eighty

Can't climb that height

To view it again

And sing to my past youthful glory

Stars and planets!

Look at it please

Read it aloud to me

The song of my youth

Engraved on the rock

The whole sky will join in

In full-throated revelry

The universe has no choice

Glory all the way petroglyphs

Wherever you are

On the surface of this earth!

103. Wailing Boy

The other day
I lay for an echo of my heart

The technician scanned my chest and sides
I could hear my heart pant aloud

Oh boy! Was that a chugging train,
a distant wail, water gurgling,
or a rhythmic rub inside an empty tub?

The guy sure was at frantic speed
wailing all the while

Thank the Lord
He has made sure
we never hear
the perturbations
of this friend of ours
labouring inside each of us
all twenty-four hours

104. Naupaka

A flower in Hawaii
blooms in halves -
half on the mounts
half on the shores.

Naupaka is its celebrated name -
we hear there was a princess of the same name
long long ago
and she fell head over heels
in love with a commoner -
a prohibited misdeed for royal ones.

The lovers went from pillar to post
to find a way out
from the quandary they were in.
They yearned to win
the heart of everyone
and live in peace as one
together for several eons.

Alas! That was not to be!
although a priest asked them to pray
at a mountain temple
to find if the Divine cared,
which with all their heart they did
without any visible aid.

Lost of hope they embraced in tears,
the princess tore the flower on her hair
into two halves and gave
one piece to her love;
she said in tears:
"Take it to the mounts my dear
and I shall return to those who least care
at the shaky shores
far down there
with the other half on my hair".

A heart-broken nuupuku plant
witnessed the event;
bleeding inside she decided
to always blossom in halves thence.

This may be a legend made up
to explain a natural wonder
of a flower blossoming in halves
but the world goes lachrymose;
humanity then sings in tears
for lovers torn asunder
on the globe everywhere..

And the winds of Hawaii
breathe this love story
day in and day out
in unceasing strains
and the stars sure do listen
as do the swaying palms.

Oh, visitor to the island, cry!
And say a prayer,
oponopono for sure,*
the Lord will listen
and lessen the pain

• "Forgive me please, I am sorry, I love you, Thank you" – that is the oponopono
prayer of Hawaii to the Lord. It takes care wherever you are.

105. Ratan Tata

You had to depart
For us to know your worth
You had to say adieu
For us to know what was our due

A man whose greatness the world didn't know
When he moved unnoticed amidst thronging crowds
And trod the earth — a silent goliath
Unconcerned with glory and wealth

Today, when you have gone
All are praise for the fortune
Of an exemplary life you taught
May that not come to naught
For we are a forgetful lot

A nation bows its head in reverence
May you, Sir, like a beacon shine
And inspire us through our Indian nights
Of ignorance and lack of foresight

Adieu! India's great son always upright
May your lessons never be a waste

www.ingramcontent.com/pod-product-compliance
Lightning Source LLC
Chambersburg PA
CBHW030804180726
47991CB00025B/1539